The Locked Chamber

Healing The Hearts of God's Daughters

Lynette M. Bradshaw

Author of: The Journey To Uncover The Real Me: Finding Myself Through God's Love

Restore her Worth

The Locked Chamber: Healing The Hearts of God's Daughters

www.RestoreHerWorth.com

First Printing, 2016

ISBN-10   0-9962292-2-1

ISBN-13   978-0-9962292-2-7

Images Copyright © 2016 by Lynette Bradshaw Photography & Lynette Bradshaw
Cover design by: Lynette M. Bradshaw
Editing by: Alana Stone Watkins
Author photographed by: Lynette M. Bradshaw, Assisted by: Charity Bradshaw

Table of Contents

Dedication

I dedicate this book to my one and only daughter, Charity. I am so blessed God allowed me to be your mother. I am even more grateful to you for being my daughter. When I look in your eyes, I see such truth, integrity, strength, creativeness and purpose.

I also look at you and see my ministry. You are the first woman God has given me to pour into. I know in order to pour into you, I must first find the strength to no longer hide behind my pain but face it head on.

Because of you, I fight daily to be a better person so I can be a greater mom. Even though you are only twelve years old, I draw tremendous inspiration and encouragement from your presence and life. You are my love and my heart. I will live my life before you knowing that you are watching me and forming your ideals of what a woman of worth, value and purpose. I take this responsibility as a privilege.

Let Us Pray Before We Begin

Father God,

Thank you for giving me the opportunity to speak my heart on these pages. Thank you for the opportunity to show your daughters through my life your love for us and your favor. I pray for each person reading these words that their hearts be pierced and encouraged to allow you into the places in their hearts that they have locked away. Father, speak to our hearts, heal our souls, and teach us to surrender the keys to The Locked Chamber, our heart. Thank you for the lives that shall be changed, renewed and transformed by your spirit as these pages are read. Let your Will be done Jesus.

In Jesus name, Amen

Acknowledgements

To my sons, Jarrius, Derrick and Adriel, I love you so much. You are an inspiration to me being the men you are. Each of you has touched a part of my heart that only you have access to. I strive daily to be an example to you of vulnerability, transformation, truth, integrity, strength and hope. God has given me to you, perfectly imperfect, but MOM. You are my joy and I am forever here for you. Thank you for being the men you are in my life. Thank you for loving me as I am and doing it unconditionally. Thank you for being the reason I keep getting back up, when nothing else seems to give me the inner strength to do so.

To my Mom-Josie M. Owens;

I love you. I have watched you live your life in pain and triumph. I am a reflection of you. I am your only daughter. I am your first born. I am thankful for it all. God gave you one daughter, and I am grateful He chose me. I may not say it enough, so I will say it now. I Am Proud of you for the woman you are. You are brave and strong. Many will never know what you have dealt with in life, but I pray that you know that you are a SURVIVOR in so many ways. I Love you Always.

To Kathy Fletcher;

Thank you for being my unchanging friend in the way you love, encourage and support me. Thank you for being you and allowing me to be me. Your friendship means the world to me. When I couldn't believe in me, you spoke a word in the right moment to give me strength to keep standing. I love you, Sunshine. I will always be your "moonglow".

To My Granddaughters, Harmony and Ja'Merria

When I stand in my purpose to empower women, I see your faces. I love you both so very much. You are the image I see, along with your aunty Charity, when I want to stop walking in my ministry. I purpose to continue to allow God to build me, strengthen me and teach me to stand in my worth so you always have an image of self- worth, value and purpose to look up to. You give me the encouragement to continue thriving to know me deeper. I thank God for your parents giving life to you and I am eternally grateful that you are part of my life.

Introduction

How many doors to your heart have been nailed shut because of the pain you have endured? You felt it you made it a vault, no one could abandon you or hurt you again. How many times has the illusion of love, the pain of abuse, the disappointment of life caused you to slam shut the doors of your heart? As God's daughters we have slammed the door of our heart and hidden the key. The keys have been hidden from the world and unfortunately hidden from God.

In my journey of self-discovery, I surprisingly discovered there are many layers to the heart of a woman. I am discovering the journey to uncover who you really are, requires you to dig deeper underneath the layers of pain, shame and silence. These are only three of the layers that hold us captive within the boundaries of our own heart. In my sophomore project, I am getting to the heart of the matter. It is the matters of the heart holding me and my sisters bound and left as victims to heartache, abandonment and more.

What are the matters? They are the wounds hidden behind the doors of the heart locking God's daughters away for safe keeping. Yet, is it really safe? The wounds are many and therefore the doors protecting them are many.

The doors to my own heart began to lose their strength as I moved deeper into my journey to discover who I Am. As I follow God further into my purpose, it awakens parts of me that gives entry to no one, not even God. How could I not give God the keys to my heart? How could I withhold parts of myself from Him? It is easy to do, when you are the keeper of your pain and the master over the entry gate of your own heart.

Sadly, the keys that I hold closely actually bind my hands. Each time I desire to walk further into my purpose and destiny, the chains tightened and hinder me in moving forward. .

Soon the heart attack begins. No, not the physical heart attack. It is the inner, soul wrenching ache in the deepest parts of the hearts of God's daughters that no man can touch or heal. Those aches lead to life suffocating you from the inside out.

As I cried out to God, without a word sometimes, I came to understand my heart was aching because of what I had locked away. I realized in order to fully embrace who I am in this stage of the journey, the doors to my heart have to be unlocked. I have to exchange bitterness for God's hand. I have to exchange suicidal thoughts for God's hand. Behind each door was the answer needed to allow my heart to be free. I needed to release the keys I held in my control to God. The weight of carrying them is why I felt suffocated in my own life. It is the reason why I felt I was hitting a stone wall each time I tried to move further in my purpose.

My sisters, it is time to dig deeper. Again, what are your matters of the heart? What do you need to release to God so your heart can function at its' full capacity? Come along with me as I share with you my secret prayers to God and gaze into the wisdom He released into my life, to bring me out of hiding to stand in my power.

God is calling His daughters into "Heart Freedom." He wants to heal the hearts of His daughters so we can no longer be held captive by the hidden wounds of our heart.

Are you okay? Are you really okay? How many times do we Stop, Look and Listen when asking this question of our sisters? If we did, she may tell you of her hidden pain that she has never been able to express or release. Many times the daughters of God are the walking wounded, waiting for a medic to come and resuscitate her even though she is living life daily. How is this possible? Because my sister, we put on our mask, dress ourselves up and cover the broken places so no one sees the shattered pieces of our heart.

Join me as I share with you the letters, my prayers, of how I finally found the courage to speak from the hidden places. I share with you how God speaks to me in those same places to help me understand how I became locked behind doors sealed with the blood of my pain, shame and silence.

I would love for you to read this book from cover to cover, yet I want you to find the chapter that speaks to you first and begin your journey. There is a section behind each chapter to write your aha moments, your breakthroughs and your transformations.

Breathe, Baby Girl. It's time sister to unlock the door of your heart and give God the keys. You have carried them too long and they are weighing you down. You no longer have to be the guardian of your heart, hoping to protect yourself from being hurt again, being bitter, being alone or being abandoned. I can identify with the heart that you protect. I tell you sister, you are not really protecting it. You are really barricading yourself, within yourself.

Before you begin, pray. Before you give up on the book, pray. Before you deny the pain that each chapter will uncover, pray. God is calling you daughter into a place of healing. No longer are you expected to be the gatekeeper of your heart. The One and Only Father has heard your prayers, your tears, and He has come to rescue you.

You are God's Daughter

No longer does the chambers of your heart have to be LOCKED...

Turn the key, open the door and allow The Father to heal the broken places within you...

Chapter 1

Her Heart's Cry

A woman's heart can endure so much and yet hide itself within her. How could my heart hold so much pain inside me? It amazes me how in this moment I could hear the chambers of my heart breaking down under the pressure of hurt, disappointment, loneliness and deep pain. At what point did I begin to lock away parts of my heart? When did I begin to deny entry to those around me as a way to protect myself? This is something only God knows. So many came and left me in the puddle of my own tears. Tears were my makeup. Tears were my constant sleeping pill. Even as a child my heart felt so broken within me. Waiting with anticipation for the next hurt or the next hateful word that would be spoken to this ugly little girl and yet hoping that it would not come. Yes, the ugly little girl that looked back at me in the mirror not only had an ugly face but she had a shattered heart to go along with it. Everyone around me made me feel so ugly and unwanted. There was simply no other way to see myself.

Each person who walked away from me, left with a part of me. They left me in pieces, shattered remnants of myself. My heart would beat yet it was without life. I would cry to God, "If you can hear me, please make them love me. I would be a good girl if you will just allow them to see me." Feeling unseen and unheard crushed the inner parts of my being. I wanted and needed someone to see my heart that was tormented within me. Teachers, family, classmates and neighbors said things to me that caused me to shrink. Did they not know I could feel their harsh words? Surely they could see my eyes when they told me my hair was a mess, that my stomach was sticking out, or laughed at me while bullying me in my face. At least I thought they could. One of my teachers added to my insecurity. No matter how hard I tried, she was always there to point out things about my hair and body. As I became older I realized they weren't even true. I developed a complex about a stomach that was flat because she would repeatedly say to me, "Suck your stomach in Lynette." For many years I saw fat around my stomach that was not even there. I can sometimes still hear her words, if only subconsciously.

The heart can break and never be seen by anyone of the natural eye. As my heart was abused, betrayed or lied to, I did not realize it stopped receiving or feeling. I have heard many times, how a person becomes numb. I became one of the numb individuals for forty plus years. I was numb to love and alive to bitterness and unhappiness. Every corner of my heart was broken in some way. It was as if my heart suffered a heart attack and everywhere that hurt touched, it turned black and no longer received a blood supply. I lived through the day trying to find someone or something to make it feel again. Whether it was a man or young boy that gave the impression that they cared for me or a new thing to try and accomplish, I dived into it like a hungry lion. I devoured any attention. I tried losing myself in a new goal so others could see that I was smart and good at something. I wanted them to recognize me.

I have learned in my 48 years of life that broken recognizes broken. Low self-esteem and low self-worth attracts the same to it. Unhappiness draws unhappiness. I needed a heart transplant because the one within my chest had lost all the ability to beat the way it was meant to. The blood flow had been hindered by pain.

As a child you do not always know what you are feeling or how to ask for what you need. Still the human soul will seek to heal and comfort itself, I used food to comfort me because no one realized a genuine hug was what I needed. I used food to be my friend. I used food to make me feel better, yet food never touched my heart. In my mind, it was more than food. It was the one thing that would not lie to me, leave me, or call me names. However, overeating food would remind me of the teacher who told me to suck in my stomach, and then the guilt would take over. My heart believed her, and I felt like I was that child again- the one she made feel fat and unattractive. A child carries so much within her little heart that she cannot express or understand. All I had become familiar with as a child were heartbreaking moments.

Eventually, the child became a woman who lived in a shell within herself. The woman would hide in the corners of her heart that could still beat if only to give her life. She learned that she could cover her brokenness with masks to show the world that she was strong and doing just fine. The truth was hidden within a locked chamber where her heart dwelled.

How can we as women live and walk around daily as living zombies. Our mouths say, "I am ok." Our body says, "Yes, I have it tight and right." Our words speak of a confident sister who does not have a worry in the world. Our lives are far from where they should be because the organ within us, that is our life source, has so many locks on it that even the deepest love cannot unlock it. Yet, we live daily hoping that someone will come along who will have a love deep enough to touch where no one ever could. We desperately want to give the key to someone who has earned it. Hunger for the words, "I love you" leads us to pull out the key. As soon as familiar words are spoken history and hurt begin to repeat itself, the lock is strengthened. In those moments, emotionally, spiritually, mentally and even physically we lock down.

A woman carries her broken heart from one relationship to another hoping this time it will be different. She has locked herself away to protect herself. Unfortunately, she does not realize that she is also locking out the love she desperately wants and deserves. She allows who and what she wants into her secret sanctuary. She knows that a key is needed in order to enter. Her secret place holds within it the images of the faces that broke her, the words that made her not love her, the failures, the doubts and tears. She is broken like a doll that needs to be glued back together. The broken places are shattered with sharp edges, uneven pieces and simply putting her back together will not be enough. Her pain, tears and bitterness rocks her to sleep at night and has sadly become her norm.

What is that beacon of light that begins to shine from within her? After many years of being a shell of who she is meant to be. She has come to a place in her life where she hears the voice of the one she never knew she was keeping out. His voice is familiar; however, the way He is calling to her now makes her uncomfortable. He is speaking to her about that special place within her where even He has not been allowed entry. Her body begins to crumble to the floor as she hears Him nudging her to let Him in. He is a gentleman and will never pressure her into doing anything against her will. Now is the time to trust that He loves her more than the pain she carries. He will never leave her. He will never betray her. He has all the love needed in one of His words that will put her back together better than ever before. His touch calms the screams within her. He shows her that the places within are in need of His blood so that it can beat to its fullest capacity. Can he really be the one that she can open up the parts of her that are held together by bandages? Can He do what a 20 year marriage could not do? Can He be trusted with all her secrets? She would have to believe and trust Him with a place that family, associates, classmates, neighbors, teachers and strangers shattered. How could she let him in this time? She realized that he had knocked on the doors of her heart many times before but she was not ready to let him in. His knocking this time caused her to weep. She somehow knew that it was time to release control. He is the only one that has shown her that giving Him the key would be the only way for her to live the life she is meant to live. He is the author and finisher of the life she is to live.

The one knocking is her Father, her daddy. He is God. He was touching her in places where others touched and caused trauma. His touch is calling to her and she is ready to answer. It is God who is knocking at her heart and asking for entry.

I was that woman. I did not realize that when I locked my heart away that I had also locked God out. I thought that if there wasn't anyone allowed into the deep places of my heart, that those places would be secure. It was a trick of satan to keep me bound and that is exactly what I had become within, bound and locked away. I was at a place in my life where the hidden places of my heart were holding me back. They were craving to be free. In order for me to live purposely and free, those doors had to be unlocked. I needed to face what was behind them.

When a person locks a door, he or she who holds the key controls access to what is behind the door. I did not want to relive the pain that was locked away. I did not want to see what I had faced in my life because my heart, my soul and my mind could not take it all at once. It would crush me. Yet, it was exactly what I needed to do in order to live. I needed to unlock the doors to my heart in order to THRIVE for the first time in my life.

I am the same as many of God's daughters who are living daily with broken and shattered hearts. The deadbolts on our hearts have protected us, or so we have thought. Our hearts hold the letters that we never wrote that expressed the years of pain and disappointment. The letters played in our subconscious and our dreams as we slept. We somehow did not even speak those words to God because the pain was too deep to uncover. As my Heavenly Father, God wanted to heal me. He wanted His daughter to fly and the locked chambers were holding me down. Are your locked chambers doing the same to you? Have you locked God out of your secret chamber, your heart?

Maybe you have been feeling God knock on the doors of your heart and have ignored the call because the pain within would be too much for your soul, mind and spirit to bear? I understand the struggle of opening up yourself to face all that is hidden behind the doors. I relate to the fear of placing the key in the hands of another person who says, "You can trust me," only to quickly have to snatch the key back again and make the lock tighter. The love they spoke about was an illusion. The love that God is speaking to you can be trusted because He is Love.

He knows His daughters are hurting. He feels our pain and turmoil. He feels our shame. He feels our cry for love. He knows we need our earthly fathers to be daddy. He sees the broken relationships between mothers and daughters. Mothers are His daughters and they are shattered. They don't know how to love and give. In turn their daughters become broken and shattered continuing the cycle.

God is waiting to hear the unwritten letters of His daughter's heart. He has a reply to each heartache, each disappointment. He has seen the way we have tried to put ourselves back together. Our way of healing ourselves will never be strong enough to unlock the walls of our heart nor heal what's hiding behind them. The key is safe with God. The key to healing His daughters is allowing Him in. His daughters are precious to Him.

Chapter 2

Are you really okay?

As Marie arrives to work, she takes a moment to compose herself in the car to prepare for the work day. All that is going on at home within her relationships and her heart rushes to the forefront of her mind. She feels suddenly heavy. She feels alone. She is thinking there is no one whom she can share her secret struggles. Her tears once again flood her eyes uncontrollably. Her tears flow not just for the current situations, but somehow came from deep within her. She felt that her heart was bleeding with pain. Time stands still in those moments as she cries wanting things to change, needing someone to not only see her but also hear her heart wanting relief from all she has endured. The pain has been a constant reminder that she was not enough. She remembers she must go inside for work. Gathering her things, she pulls herself together. Carefully she wipes her eyes, corrects her makeup and puts on her smile that says, "I am just fine." Yet, she knows that she is far from it.

Marie walks into the break room in her office deep in thought practically ignoring everyone and everything around her. She says good morning to her co-worker, Faith. Faith says, "Hi girl, how are you?" Marie replies, "I am good, how are you?" Faith begins telling Marie about her weekend, how great her daughter performed at her recital and the great surprise her husband had for her when she arrived home on Friday. Faith never notices that Marie has gotten lost in her own burdens in that moment. She never notices that Marie is hearing what she is saying, but she is not listening. Faith, like many of us, asked her sister how she was, yet she never stopped, looked or listened. Had she done so, she would have noticed that even though Marie said she was "Good," she was nowhere near it.

How many times do we ask others "How are you" and actually stop, look and listen? If we would do that, then we could ask, "Marie are you really good? Marie are you really okay?" Doing so could be the support she needs to release her heart issues and burdens to someone who cares for her. Even if she can only share parts of her story in that moment, it could take the pressure off of her on the inside to where she no longer feels as though she will explode. She is screaming for help. The question, "How are you?" can be the words someone hurting is waiting to hear. A simple hug, a moment of someone listening would remind her that she is not alone and that others care for her. The question, "How are you," is a loaded one that has the potential to change a life.

Women go through life-changing moments. She learns over time to just say, "I am okay." Saying she is okay has become the acceptable response when her heart is breaking into pieces. The silent storms she lives with can be invisible to others. She is struggling with depression. She is overwhelmed with anxiety. She fears she will fail again. She fears she will not be enough because she feels insignificant. She feels shame because she was sexually abused. The marriage that everyone believes is amazing because of the illusion she has given, is now in divorce court. Her husband who she has portrayed to others as loyal, honest and loving has already entered into a new relationship, and she is engulfed with pain. Her childhood pain of being abandoned seems to show up in every relationship. She smothers those she loves and who show they have some concern for her in hopes that they too will not leave her. Resentment shows her that all men are the same, according to what she has experienced. Jealousy will not allow her to see that she is as good as the woman who has long hair, big legs and the perfect shape. She remembers how others in her past criticized her no matter what size she was. She carries the pain of others tormenting her because her hair was short and unhealthy. She feels ugly. She feels unwanted. She feels alone and yet when asked, she boldly and without thought says, "I'm fine." Her heart is no longer functioning as it should because of all that she is carrying. She has yet to realize that part of her internal being is dying away spiritually and emotionally, primarily her heart.

In the break room at work, at that party, in that conversation, the simple question of "How are you?" creates a facade by which the wounded answer. My sisters are hurting and hiding behind lies thinking it will help her to make it through the day. The lies become masks to protect and distract from what she is really going through inside. In my last book, *"The Journey to Uncover The Real Me: Finding Myself Through God's Love,"* I spoke about the masks that I have worn since child hood to get others to like me, to love me, to want me but mostly to protect myself. It became my life security. Eventually my hurt would be used as manipulation to get attention. However, my real issue was my heart was broken and shattered, and I needed someone to care enough to see me, really see me. I spoke of how I lived life not really living but being- who I thought I needed to be in order to get what my heart and soul desperately needed. I lived a lie because to me it was my truth. For many years my heart could not and would not feel. It beat daily because I was alive; however, living was totally opposite. From childhood, parts of my heart were locked away. Each disappointment, betrayal, hurt, loss and traumatic event I endured put my heart in a position to shut down, break down and go into hiding. Sadly, I did not realize that my heart had become anesthetized in many ways. As I began my journey to uncover the "Real Me," I came to realize this journey would open up some deep places within my heart that were locked away from others, me and mostly God.

I am Marie. Are you? What is your heart needing? The journey to heal is not an easy one. The journey to find your truth is not easy. Yet it is necessary. You have not arrived at this moment by chance. As I have, you have come to a place in your journey that God is showing there are places within you that are hidden. This is your moment. You are here to begin the next stage of your journey and it is amazing. It really shows that God has heard your prayers. He has felt your pain. He has captured your tears. He has an appointed time to deal with the issues of our heart that no one has been privy to. We have shared with the world and God parts of our struggle, and this is awesome. Yet, there are wounds that cause our hearts to be shut down and they over shadow our lives. This is the part of us where we must go and invite Him in.

Love is a powerful tool. It is a masterful emotion meaning it is the source from which we learn all things. God is love. Love restores. God is a restorer. Love transforms pain into passion, pain into healing, and pain into purpose. Even though the outer part of my sisters look all together, in order to allow Love to do its' purpose in your life, you must go within yourself and dig deeper into the ground of your heart. Are we listening to our sisters, our co-workers, daughters, mothers and friends? Maybe we aren't able to listen to them because we ourselves are not listening to our own hearts. Have you created a shield and closed off your heart so much that now you are disconnected from it? What is your heart speaking to you? What are you refusing to unlock in your own heart that has caused you to walk with a mask that speaks to the world that you are just fine? When our heart is filled with pain we can lose the ability to see anyone's state of being because ours is tainted. So here we are locked in our pain and our sisters are locked in theirs.

Love is available to each of us as we proceed on our journey to heal and discover who we are. The journey will lead to love which, in turn, leads us to see ourselves. It will allow us to deal with our wounds so we are able to reach back for our sisters and assist them along their journey. It is a heart issue, and it is time to get to the heart of the matter. Do not worry that it will be too much for you. As I have walked my journey of self-discovery, God has allowed me to discover piece by piece of where I was wounded. God knows what we are able to handle at any given stage of our journey. The wounds of the heart go deep and wide. God is doing surgery in His daughters. If you will trust Him in this process, you will no longer be anesthetized as you walk through life. Instead you will not only feel but have the capacity to help your sister unlock the issues of her heart to begin to do the same.

I remember many years ago when God spoke to me this revelation. He showed me that in the center of "Heart" is the word "Ear." I understood back then what He was showing me in this truth. Now I understand it differently because I see my heart needing to hear His Word that says, "As a man thinketh so is he."(Proverbs 23:7) In my heart for many years I thought I was insignificant, unloved and unwanted. I believed I was only meant to be hurt. I felt abandoned and I grabbed hold to people in dire need of them to stay. My heart was locked because I chose to close it off without even realizing what I was doing. Our hearts should hear beyond the answer "I am okay" that comes from our sisters and mostly from our own lips. As we hear and listen we must find the courage to go deeper. Going deeper has scared God's daughters for many years and because of that many have walked around only existing in public and being tormented in private. They have been afraid to touch the place in them that only they are allowed to visit. They find the courage and strength to take a peek inside and when they do they find there is so much pain they cannot breathe. They again close the door and lock it away. God's daughters have hearts that are screaming, "I am struggling and barely keeping my head above water." Their hearts are crying, "I do not know how to live and feel as if no one likes me or loves me any longer." They do not know how to tell anyone that the pain is so bad, that they do not want to live anymore with the pain that the events in her life have brought her. She watches and waits, hoping someone will care enough to hear her heart and allow God to lead them to stop and listen to what her answer is really hiding.

Are you that woman who is crying and screaming out from within for relief? Are you drowning in the oozing of your wounds because you are afraid to unlock the issue of your heart so you can not only live but thrive? I realize that God is showing me that I am this woman. I am at a stage of the journey where the key must be used to unlock the door that holds the pain that I have never trusted to anyone, not even God. We have not trusted Him with pain so deep it was never to be spoken of. We believed even God can not cure what has caused us to be sick emotionally and yet He says, "There is balm in Gilead." (Jeremiah 8:22) We seem to always be on a quest to dig deeper within ourselves in order to walk in the power of who God birthed us to be. It is not a punishment. It is God answering our prayers to heal and move forward. In order for that to be done, the old things within us, the pain and the masks must first be confronted, dealt with and released one step at a time.

Breathe Baby Girl, daddy is here. Remember God is a gentleman and will not push you to open up this precious part of yourself. He wants you to know you can Trust Him with the hidden chambers of your heart that have been locked, bound and uninviting. Daddy is reaching his hand to you and if you were not ready to walk with Him at this stage of your journey, believe me you would not be here. Be strong and of good courage (Joshua 1:9) because He will be with you always. He will be with you every step you take. Breathe Baby Girl and know that your heart is valuable to God. It is your secret place but you no longer have to hold him at bay. He is not the parent or parents that abused you. He is not the relative that touched you where he shouldn't have. He is not the bully who made you feel low and unwanted. He is Abba Father and His Love will penetrate the deepness of you to bring forth all that He purposed for you. As He is allowed into the rooms that hold many years of pain, you are able to walk into your purpose whole and complete. Are you ready to proceed? Remember to Breathe Baby Girl, and hold tight. It is time…

Ask yourself these questions before you proceed:

Am I really okay?

_____

Am I hiding behind the door of my heart?

_____

Am I ready to give God the key to the door of my secret chamber?

_____

Am I ready to face my truth behind the door?

_____

Chapter 3

Her Hidden Place

The heart of a woman is a place where she can hide her pain, express her deepest love, cover her greatest fear and lock it away. When you touch the heart of a woman, you must know that next to her soul and her spirit, that you have touched a secret place that many may never have access to. Yet, for most women giving that key to those who didn't understand what love is, who only wanted to misuse her generous ability to love or sent their representative to deceive her leaves her broken and fearful to be vulnerable again. The sweetest part of her can become the bitterest place within her. Out of our hearts should flow rivers of Living Water (John 7:38), but when life brings hurt, abandonment, fear, a breaking of trust and more, she has learned to shut down the life source within her.

Our hearts have been clogged with fear, pain, bitterness, unforgiveness, insecurity, desperation for love, fear of being hurt, abandonment, betrayal and sickness among many things. What we actually do is stop the heart chamber from receiving the life giving blood of God to touch those places within our life giving organ, the heart. As women we sometimes become walking shells of who we are meant to be due to what our hearts have endured. There are times when the pain we have has felt is so deep, it literally feels like our hearts are breaking in two. In order to protect our hearts from ever feeling this type of pain again, we emotionally, mentally and spiritually shuts down our systems. This system is our heart function. It no longer can flow with rivers of living water because of words and images within it that exude sewage. Out of our mouths flows the residue of what pain has left.

I was amazed when God began to show me the heart through my work in my career as a Medical Assistant in Cardiology. God takes the simple and sometimes overlooked things of life to give us revelation in order that we can come out of bondage into freedom. His love for us is so great. He knows the trails that we have followed and the journey's we've lived from childhood to this moment. Our hearts beat with life and yet it is dying as the plaque of bitterness, rage, hurt, and so much more stops us from living in the happiness we deserve.

The heart is a small organ made up of four chambers, valves and arteries that work in a way to allow the blood to flow in one direction. Sometimes depending on diet, lack of exercise, and other health conditions, the heart can malfunction. The flow of the cycle that begins the heart to beat goes through many small and large arteries and valves. The blood flow is meant to go in one direction. Whenever something within the heart malfunctions and causes the flow to go backwards or one of the chambers to beat at the wrong time, the heart cannot allow the body to function correctly. It can bring weakness. It can cause some areas to be blocked. The disruption causes the electrical current that allows the chambers of the heart to start and stop as it should not to operate properly. This small organ is the life source of God's children. It is a small yet powerful source of energy that allows the runner to sprint down the track and a child to feel joy when daddy walks through the door. When I think of how pain, heartbreak, abandonment and bitterness affect the spiritual heart, I am able to see how we are unable to function to full capacity with these afflictions. Each time those wounds are inflicted; they cause the heart to break into pieces. Sometimes it causes a minor cut and for others the wound is so intense it feels like a major heartache that shuts down every chamber immediately and dies away. It is mind blowing how powerful this is. God wants His girls to heal and since the heart is the life source within the human body and yet the spiritual pump that causes the body to thrive, it is the perfect place to begin transformation.

Although all of God's children are born with this organ, it is to His daughters that I am speaking to

in this moment. Being one of His daughters, I
know first-hand how the chambers of our heart
can and does shut down and malfunction within.
When this happens, the daughters of God become
walking chambers of stone without even knowing
it. She speaks words covered in defense. She
reacts with paranoia. She speaks with words
clotted with bitterness. She is determined that no
one will get close enough to her to see her
damaged heart nor feel the love that is waiting to
be revived within it. Within each girl and woman
there is a place where all her joyful and hurtful
moments abide. Within this place she can choose
to withhold or release herself. Far too many times
she chooses to lock this place away. For many it is
never opened. Within this place, she holds the key
to the door where only she knows its' existence
and its location. She has become so accustom to
shielding herself, that she does not understand
her shielding is also hurting her. Her heart has
been shattered into pieces and bandaged back
together with her tears and anger. Each time her
heart is betrayed, broken, abused or lied to, pieces
of it cracks open and it has begun to turn to stone
within her. In order to allow it to heal, she must
allow herself to be vulnerable. Vulnerability to

her says that she has to take the risk of being hurt again and that is a price that she refuses to pay. The pain would be too great to bear.
Transparency suggest that nothing is hidden and everything is available to be seen to the naked and spiritual eye. Yet, vulnerability requires trust to let down ones guards and allow someone into those places that are carefully protected.

Do you remember that you are God's daughter? Wow, that is such a beautiful identity to have. However; to know this and to feel this truth is sometimes so far apart. For some, this truth brings up the truth that I'm my daddy and mamma's daughter too. The thought immediately is covered in pain and abandonment. The thought that God could possibly love you the way you were loved as a child can bring fear and pain. Those thoughts can stop you in your tracks. The great truth is that God's love for you cannot be compared to anyone else in your life. His love will heal the places within that the illusion of love caused to break.

Can you recognize her within yourself? She is hidden underneath multiple college degrees, makeup, insecurity, bitterness, loneliness that have become her identity and her heartbeat. Many will deny that anything is wrong with them because that would mean she would need to be vulnerable. Are you her? Is your heart functioning to full capacity or have you bandaged it up with your tears and patched it with your pain as glue for the perfect art project? The little girl within needs to breathe and heal her secret chambers and come out from behind the false sense of security she has created. God has seen your patch work of your heart and He can do far better for you. He has seen the damage that life has caused to your heart. He wants to speak to the hidden places and cause the blood to flow into those places once again. He wants you to know that you deserve a heart that is not patched with illusions of healing, but love, compassion and comfort so it can allow the energy and fullness of life to flow from you.

In the natural heart, when the arteries are clogged a person can begin to have dizziness, fainting, shortness of breath or other symptoms. In the spiritual heart we can lose the ability to breathe because we are smothering from the pain stopping the flow of God's anointing, His love and His healing within us. No longer do we have to walk with stones in our heart where the blood tries to flow but it is hindered and in response to that we are seen as angry, shy, bitter, deceptive or worse. No longer do we have to live out of the residue of pain. By turning the key to your closed door and giving God the key, you can allow light to enter where only darkness has dwelled and controlled.

Eventually as I began to discover who I was underneath the pain, I realized I could unlock another door of my heart and give God the key to another part of me. As I share the chambers of my heart, I also share the unspoken pain of my sisters as I see them walking in a shell of who they are meant to be. As sisters we are each other's keeper. We are all hiding something. We have been seeking the one person, career and accomplishment that will be the answer to the pain of the past.

I want to share with you my letters that were unspoken except within my own mind and in my moments of despair. While learning to trust God with the key to my pain, I realized I would have to face me. Yes, me. You see, behind every locked door of my heart was a part of me that was being locked and boarded up. The lock was to keep the pain from being felt and from anyone inflicting the same.

Are you ready to begin? In order to allow the flow of the heart and the function of the heart in its spiritual form and natural form to work properly, we must carefully deal with what is there holding us in place. As we proceed forward in the following chapters, I pray that you will discover through the letters to God where you have locked your heart away. In order for us to deal with trauma that is there, we have to be willing to be vulnerable enough to be honest with ourselves and God. As I write from my own perspective and from the perspective of other women I have encountered, I know we can slowly and carefully unlock the hidden chambers within our own hearts. It will not be easy. God will show you as you read where you are hiding in your heart so that He can bring healing to that place. The letters that precede each chapter are prayers you can pray out loud to God or add your own prayers in place of them. The purpose of the letters is to begin the process of unlocking the chambers that are not allowing blood to flow. The blood supply comes through God's love. As the life supply from His love touches those places, you will begin to see yourself blossom and thrive. What we lock away becomes dead. God can not heal what is hidden. Although He knows what we need, where we are hurting, it is a position of trust to freely turn those places over to Him. It is also a position of surrender to Him showing that you can trust Him with your deepest pain. Before you proceed answer the coaching questions below as honestly as possible. You are capable of so much more than you have believed. Use your key of permission to turn the lock to the door that has been sealed with the years of pain that was too deep for you to face. Behind that door may be bitterness, unforgiveness, shame, self-hate, distrust, low self-esteem, abandonment and more.

My prayer is, in one or more of these letters, you can find where you are and find the strength to allow God to be the key to your healing. My sister, what is your letter from your heart chamber? What is your cry? What is your pain point? Are you ready for the bitterness, anger, fear, doubt, shame, etc. to stop screaming from within you? God wants to heal His daughters' hearts and that includes you.

It's your time sister. Let's turn the key......It's Time to Dig Deeper:

Ask the Holy Spirit to reveal to you the three areas in your life that you have locked away and need healing....

_____

_____

_____

Chapter 4

A Heart of Bitterness

Dear God,

My heart is filled with anger, rage and bitterness. God they have continually hurt me and I don't know how to feel anymore. My heart is covered in rage where there should be love. How can I let anyone into my heart again and risk being hurt? I try to understand how I arrived in this place. Was it at the moment when he cheated on me? Was it at the moment when he left? Maybe it does not have anything to do with him. I know this bitterness is deep within me. Maybe you can help me understand? My heart is hardened with bitterness when all I want to do is give love and myself to others. I remember when I was younger and I simply loved everyone. It came so easy. Now that idea scares me. The moments when my life changed are overwhelming. Oh God, could those moments really be the reason? God you said that I can cast all my cares on you, right? So does that include when they touched me in my secret place? Does it also include the pain of trusting them when they said they loved me but treated me like I was scum under their shoes? No, God I don't believe it was those moment. I think it was when I told my mother, and she did not listen to me. As a little girl, I said it the way I thought she would understand. I told God and nothing changed. I hurt so bad that my heart felt as if it would crash through my chest. I was just a little girl, why didn't anyone help me? Each time I saw my family members I was enraged. They never penetrated me physically, but they penetrated me spiritually and emotionally. Why, God? As I grew into a teenager, the touching started to decrease. Was it because I wasn't good enough anymore? That made me angry to even think this way, even though I wanted it to stop. I became angry with myself because I felt that way. Then I became angry because I wanted it all to go away. My heart muscles were competing with one another. One part of my heart wanted to hate and the other wanted to love. I felt so confused. God I need help. My anger is overtaking me. It is controlling my moments. It is stealing my peace. The people around me see a raging bull of a person who destroys everything in its view. Can't they see I'm hurting? Why won't they help me, Lord? I don't know, maybe it's because they only see the rage and hear the bitterness. Lord, I still remember the moments as a girl when my body was rubbed against by the person who was my family. I did not know what to feel other than fear. I could not protect myself. I had to live daily fearful that he would come again and he did. His touch was no longer cousin. His touch was no longer family friend. His touch, yes his touch, it brought with it chains. Those chains locked my heart in that moment. He does not represent one, but many. As I grew up and I would see my mommy's face, I felt hurt that she didn't protect me. Then I thought, maybe the same thing happened to her. O well, that doesn't excuse the fact that she did not protect me from them. Wasn't she supposed to help me, Lord? So here we are, Lord. I'm at my breaking point. I need you. My heart can no longer take the weight of this bitterness. I am bitter and it affects every part of me. It is as a flesh-eating organism that is without boundaries and kills everything it touches. God, please help me. I can trust you, right? You said I can. I've told you my secret. Will you rescue me? I know I am a woman now, but the little girl within me is still in that moment. I don't know what to do anymore. I want to be happy. The little girl within me wants to be happy. Can you rescue us from our bitter prison? My heart needs you. I need you. I am reaching out to you through a heart that doesn't know anything but fear. Fear has created anger, and anger has birthed bitterness. I know I'm ready now to exchange my heart of bitterness for a heart of peace. I'm casting all my cares on you, so my moment can be new. I want to move out of the moments that held me captive into a moment I can breathe. Yes Lord, I can't breathe. Just like I held my breath waiting for someone to save me then, I am still holding my breath. Help me, Jesus.

Signed,

A Daughter of Bitterness

Bitterness is the evidence of unhealed anger birthed from pain. Bitterness is fueled by pain. Within our heart we locked away that part of us that others saw as vulnerable enough to hurt us. God knows where you have hidden your pain because there wasn't anyone protecting you. You were hurt in ways that a little girl was never meant to be hurt. You are bitter as a woman because you still search for someone to protect you. As you speak to others now all they hear is bitter when you are simply using it as a shield. That place within your heart is turning to stone, and God is saying to cast your cares upon Him. Bitterness is the result. In order to heal that place, the wound in your heart, which is the root of it, is actually what needs to be touched. That is the part in the journey where we normally turn back because the root of bitterness is hurt. What has hurt you so deeply that you found yourself in fear of allowing anyone to touch that place again? Whatever you have endured that caused you hurt, it is not greater that God and you can trust Him.

Bitterness is like poison. It is like acid. It eats away at everything it touches. Sometimes we remain bitter waiting for the one who caused the hurt to apologize. We hope one day they will see what they have done and the effect it has on our lives and show remorse. This may never come. Are you willing to live your life never allowing bitterness to be replaced with love because you are waiting on someone else to help you heal? You deserve so much more. Releasing bitterness is up to you, not the one who hurt you.

As with every wound, bitterness must be acknowledged that it exist within you. It will not and cannot be overcome if it is not first acknowledged that it is a part of you. As you think of poison and acid you can begin to see how it burns within you eating away at the goodness of your heart and causing it to die away. Bitterness comes from bitter, and bitter comes from unsettled pain and turmoil. Bitterness is pain turned inward. It is the feeling of guilt that lingers after disappointment. Your heart is locked within itself, and the arteries are closing with the rocks of bitterness that you turn within yourself. It is up to you to turn the key to the root of the bitterness. Bitterness is the result but the pain and betrayal is the root. Are you ready to release the poison from your heart? You no longer have to turn inwardly because of what you have been through. The Bitterness needs to be released but first you must be willing to be vulnerable enough to allow God to be the keeper of your heart and you. He is calling to you, sis. Do you hear Him? The bitterness is blocking your heart and ears from hearing The Father calling to His daughter. I hear His voice speaking softly to us as we fight and resist Him. Yet, His voice is finally able to break through and you are ready to receive. He's calling to you now, listen and feel Him within the deepest parts of your pain...

God is saying to you,

"My daughter you have stirred and wrestled with your bitterness and anger for too long." I have watched you try and build a shield around you of anger and rage. My daughter you are broken and battered in your spirit daily. Do you understand why those around you pull away? Do you not see those who love you are tired of taking your wrath? I am here for you.

I am your Comforter (John 14:16). I am the One
who will heal you (Exodus 15:26). The person
that others see is not the daughter that I see. I
hear your tears and feel your pain. You blame
yourself for the betrayal. You are angry because
those you trusted did not rescue you. In their own
pain they were unable to hear you with their inner
ear. They heard you speak the words they had
spoken themselves and found the same result
from others not believing them or protecting
them. You are my daughter and I no longer want
you to carry this burden within you. Your
bitterness is residue of your pain that says
somehow you deserved to be hurt. It tells you that
you are not wanted and so you were tossed aside.
This is not so. If you will trust Me, I will rescue
you from the cave of your own heart. I know that
you have carried this bitterness for many years
hoping that someone would say, "I'm sorry."
Those words may never come. How much of your
life are you willing to give to unspoken pain? How
many more moments will you give to a broken
heart that is unwilling to relinquish bitterness and
in return receive peace? You my daughter are a
precious jewel in my sight. Your heart can not
carry the weight of your anger anymore. You have

fought long and hard on your own. I have stood and watched you live daily as a roaring lion to those who were close and at night crying yourself to sleep. Your broken pieces have began to show and your tough exterior has begun to crumble. Your body is tired from the pressure of the bitter fumes filling your entire being each time you spit poison with your words. You want those around you to come near and hold you, yet your venomous words cause the opposite effect.

"My daughter your keys to your heart have held you in captivity with bitterness. I Am here to rebuild all that bitterness has eaten away. Every corner that it has turned to darkness, I will bring light. First you must see what is behind your doors. Bitterness has seemed to be the roaring lion that was the keeper of your doors. It not only kept anyone from entering but it has kept you bound as well."

"I want you, my daughter, to release bitterness to Me as it no longer serves you. Bitterness has lost its power and strength within you. It is your time to breathe. Bitterness has caused your breathing to be shallow and your pulse to race. You are constantly on guard and ready for battle as you believe that everyone will try to find your vulnerable place and bring more hurt.

It is your time now. Your weakened heart is showing you that the guardian of your wounds no longer is comfort to you. If you are ready to allow me to be God in your broken places, I will give you the freedom you rightly deserve. Will you trust Me? Will you exchange your bitterness for My peace? Will you exchange your rage for my comfort? Strength and hope will guard your heart, and roaring will no longer be against you or others, but it will be for you. My daughter it is time for you to rest in Me. It is time for you to rest your battle gear and replace it with mine. You are my soldier and you are wounded. I am here to go behind the door of your heart and unwrap the scabbed over wounds and bring a fresh and eternal healing that your heart has been waiting for. Take my hand and walk with Me, and we shall unlock the chambers together. Breathe, Baby Girl. Daddy is here and you are safe."

Scriptures Regarding Bitterness:

Deuteronomy 29:18

18: So that there may not be among you man or woman or family or tribe, whose heart turns away today from the Lord our God, to go and serve the gods of these nations, and that there may not be among you a root bearing bitterness or wormwood;

1 Samuel 1:10

10: And she was in bitterness of soul and prayed to the Lord and wept in anguish.

Job 21:25

25: Another man dies in the bitterness of his soul, never having eaten with pleasure

Proverbs 14:10

10: The heart knows its own bitterness, and a stranger does not share its joy

Ephesians 4:31

31: Let all bitterness, wrath, anger, clamor and evil speaking be put away from you, with all malice.

Reflection:

Chapter 5

The Heart of a Motherless Daughter

Dear God

My heart and soul aches for her. Even as a grown woman, the little girl within me still longs for her. You said she gave me what she was given. It is all she knows. Sadly, that doesn't change how her words tore through my soul. Those words I wrestle with every day trying to prove to myself that this is not who I am. Her voice in our house as a child was loud, mean and controlling. I came to hate the sound of it. I felt smothered from the inside out. Mommies are supposed to be sweet, right? All I felt was bitter. She's my mommy, but I feared her. I later came to resent her. I didn't deserve her rage. Why couldn't she try to love me? Why did she not like me? I felt like I was a burden to her. I felt I reminded her of something bad or wrong. Each time she looked at me I felt like an out of place item that she did not want. God my heart is closed to her, and I do not know how to open it now. My heart is buried and hidden. Her words declaring love now do not penetrate. Her declaration of being proud of me does not speak to me. Where there should be softness within me for her, there is hardness. I want her. I need her. God why didn't you teach her to love me? Why didn't you show her I was hurting? You knew what I needed. Her words cut my soul deep. Her lack of love moved me to search for love in anyone available. Other women, other mothers, I longed for them to love me. I grew to a woman with a spirit and heart of a little girl. I smothered women who were my friends and I wanted to keep them away from everyone else. My friendships were mother-daughter relationships instead of friendships. I pushed them all away. I did not understand why the women I called friends would walk away. It was like being rejected by mom over and over again. I now understand the heaviness of my friendship to them. I understand why they pushed me away. They did not deserve that. I gave them me in hopes they would say, "Baby girl, mommy loves you." They could not replace mommy for me. God, my heart still breaks for her. I feel motherless. I feel orphaned and I am not. My heart will feel for her in small bits. When I am in her presence it locks down. The anger, resentment, unforgiveness, distrust and rage became the wall that covers my heart. It is my protection that she will not get inside and bring more pain. God help me. I do not want these rocks within me for mommy. You said we are to honor our mother (Exodus 20:12). There is no honor in my wall I have built against her. God do you hear me? Can you feel my cry? The places where my love for mom should dwell is dry and untouchable.

The little girl within is in the corner needing a rescue. I see her sitting with her knees up to her chest, her head in her hands holding herself tight. She is waiting for the love she can only get from mommy to heal her. God will you save me from this hidden place? My inner child needs to know that it is ok to let go and let love in. In her ponytails and barrettes she does not know how to play and be at peace. Will you teach her to swing around in circles with her hands outstretched with a smile on her face that comes from a well of love overflowing from deep within her soul? Allow us to become one. Teach us to love mommy in spite of what she has or has not done. Mommy is also motherless. Mommy is orphaned. Allow my heart to feel her, accept her and have compassion towards her. God heal me as I stretch to love the one who did not know how to love me. My love for you is what I need to break down the doors that hide the place within that mommy did not know how to touch. I am reaching out from behind that door asking You to come and rescue me. Rub my hair and hold me close. Allow the rocks to fall away and restore my heart that beats with love. No longer shall I be orphaned because You said I am accepted in the Beloved (Ephesians 1:6). You God are my Beloved.

Signed,

A Motherless Daughter

Mothers and daughters sometimes have special relationships. They sometimes look as mirror images of each other in their features, personalities and dreams and sometime they are total opposites. The relationships can be beautiful, honorable and respectful and sometimes they are not. As a mother myself, I also want the loving, trusting, respectful and understanding between my daughter and I. My upbringing and personal struggles remind me that in order to have this special bond with her, I will have to choose to work towards this goal daily. I will have to push through my own shortcomings, lack of knowledge and insecurities in order to be able to give to her what she rightfully deserves.

There are those of us who feel as motherless daughters even when our mothers have raised us and are still a part of our lives. As adults we still interact with them and they are alive and well. Yet the little girl within us hungers for her. Even when you come to a place of accepting your mother for who she is and forgiving her for what she could not give to you, did not know how to give to you or chose not to give to you, the longing for the mother-daughter relationship remains within. It can be very painful at times to see other mothers and daughters having beautiful relationship and wonder why you cannot or could not have the same.

I am quick to say that in every relationship there are birthing periods, healing periods and a time to come to a common understanding of each other. There aren't any perfect relationships regardless of how they look on the outside. Some relationships that we take notice of and decide this is what we want for ourselves, may have taken many years to get to a place of mutual respect and love.

The mother-daughter relationship is no different than any other. There is give and take. It is a process. Some mothers raise their daughters as they were raised and never take the time to evaluate and assess what is good or bad to pass along to their child. Just because it is what we know does not mean that it is right for another individual, especially our child. As we pass along our upbringing, beliefs and understanding to our daughters it is important we look at the full picture. The full picture allows us to see the parts of our relationships that caused us to be broken in our self-image, confidence and worth. Ignoring this important part of the relationships can continue the cycle of brokenness in our own daughters. This can happen primarily because we do not know better. The saddest part is when we choose to not know better.

God wants to heal and restore the parts of us that continue to feel motherless. God's Word says He will not abandon us even if our mothers do and He will hold us close (Psalm 27:10). To me this says to my heart that God will fill the places that feel motherless. He will hold us close and whatever is or has lacked in our relationships with our moms, He will fill. God knows when His daughters have not received what is needed to feel like a mothered child. He knows what is needed to heal the void.

The pain endured, the rejection given, and the fear felt is the reason the motherless child has locked her heart away. You have closed your heart off to your mother. Your heart has been closed off also to other women. It amazes me how the relationship with our moms can cause us to see all women around us in the same way. Immediately there is the lack of trust because in them you see mom. It is not fair to other women to be in this position. You have not dealt with your own wounds and your vision is not clear. It is actually tainted. It keeps you from having beautiful relationships with the different women in your life from your co-workers, family members and more. The women you come in contact with do not realize that you see them as a repeat of what you have always known regarding women, trusting them and not being able to depend on them.

Yet all I can say is, "But God". God knows you are in a place of being ready to face and deal with the broken part of your heart that desires your mother to be the mother you need or wanted. He knows that you really do not know how to trust Him with this place inside of you. He knows that you believe that if you unwrap this wound that it will be an unbearable pain. However, it is the same courage to open that pain and wound that will allow you to be free.

God wants you to know……

God says, "I was there." I was there before you were born and when you were born. I was there when you were wounded and rejected. I was there when you were looked over. I know I see the woman you have become but I still feel the daughter who is in pain. It is not easy. However, I have felt your pain. I took it all within me on the cross. I took it all within myself so when you were strong enough and brave enough to give your pain over to me , I could feel everything you have been holding on to all your life. When you look in the mirror seeing the woman staring back at you, you refuse to look in her eyes because you dare not venture into knowing what is really behind them. You cover yourself with the prettiest clothes and the smoothest makeup and the many degrees in hope that it will take away or even numb you from the inside out. However, those are exterior elements, and they will never have what is needed to take away the internal yearning nor the pain of your past. Again, you see the woman, but I feel the little girl. I behold the little girl who feels she had to mother herself because her mother was not able to do so. The little girl within who feels motherless because her mother chose drugs, men, sex, etc. over her daughter is crying out. You feel bitter, loneliness, anger and abandonment because your mother did not know how to give you more than what she was given. Yes, your mother gave what was given to her. Sadly, it was not enough. Each time she chose not to be who I called her to be, she wounded and victimized you. She is a victim as much as you are. It does not excuse her from the responsibility for the pain she has caused. Yet, there is something that you must now see and know. Your mother is also a broken little girl. She was reaching out of herself hoping to find love, acceptance and someone to tell her that she was loved and meant it. As your mother looked at you, the little girl within her rebelled. You became her enemy whether she knew it or said it. You were a reflection of who she was on the inside. As you have learned, my daughter, it is not always easy to gaze at your reflection. It is easier to pretend it does not exist and simply turn away.

Here you are my daughter, ready, maybe not. You are second guessing yourself about going forward. I know where you are in this moment. I Am here for you. I have been waiting for you to trust me with your pain and lay your head in my arms and allow me to be what your mother was unable to be for you. The little girl within you rebels when she sees her mother. Her anger is seen. Her anger is heard. Most of all her cry for mommy is heard. You are all grown up. You want so desperately to live as an adult woman. You desire to be brave and strong. It does not mean that you are not. However, you are walking crippled because the little girl within you is sitting in the corner pouting. She is asking, "Why do I have to go through this? She is asking, "Why does she not love me?" She is asking, "Why can't she be there for me?" She wants to be the child in the relationship with her mom and allow her mom to be the mom because the roles have been switched.

Well, daughter, today is that day. It is time for you to come out of the corner of your life where you have been waiting for your mother to come and rescue you or apologize to you for the hurt she has caused you. This may never happen. Remember, she is also hurting. She is also turning away from the mirror. She is also hiding from what's really inside. You are not her rescuer and neither is she yours. I Am your Father. I know the pain of you both. If you will trust Me in this moment with the key to the damaged place within your heart, I will come in and I will be your rescuer. I will be your restorer. No longer do you have to be motherless. I will heal the wounds inside that cry out for a mother who can give you what you need or what you want. If you will give Me the keys, I will come in and heal all wounds that are oozing. You know the wounds I speak of, right? They tell you that you are worthless because your mother did not love you. Those same wounds shout to you that you are insignificant because your mother did not want to hear what you had to say and never allowed your voice to be heard. You remember the wounds that you have scabbed over enough by shopping, overeating, having sex with enough people and numbing yourself with alcohol. These wounds do not have to cry out to you anymore. You no longer have to use the substitutions of natural things to heal yourself because they are only causing you to be increasingly broken. I know that you are ready. I know that you may be hesitant in giving me the keys. You have kept them so secure. It is your way to convince yourself you are in control of something concerning your mom. You have chosen not to forgive her because in your mind it is your way of making her hurt the way she has hurt you. Sadly, the truth is this has only caused the lock on your heart to become stronger. It has caused you to become more victimized.

Are you ready to come into the conqueror and warrior that you are despite the relationship with your mom? I called you to be someone that is only uncovered as you begin to trust me. Continuing to live as the little girl instead of the woman you are, with all her broken and shattered places will hinder you in unveiling your true purpose. Regardless of you living all these years as a motherless daughter and acting out of that, I still see greatness in you. I still see your purpose in you. It is waiting for you to come in search of it. It is also locked behind the door of your heart.

Are you ready? Are you ready my daughter? I know that you are ready because I knew this day would come. Open the door to me and allow me to come in so that we can begin your restoration, healing and elevation. It is all waiting for you behind the door. Take my hand and walk with me and allow your little girl to be free.

Scriptures for Motherless Daughters-Comfort:

Psalm 138:3

3: In the day when I cried out, You answered me, and made me bold with strength in my soul

Romans 10: 17

17: So then faith comes by hearing and hearing by the Word of God

Psalm 147:3

3: He heals the brokenhearted and binds up their wounds.

Psalm 34:18-19

18: The Lord is near to those who have a broken heart, and saves such as have a contrite spirit

19: Many are the afflictions of the righteous, but the Lord delivers him out of them all

Matthew 11:28-29

28: Come to Me, all you who labor and are heavy laden, and I will give you rest

29: Take My yoke upon you and learn from Me, for I Am gentle and lowly in heart and you will find rest for your souls

Reflection:

_____

_____

_____

_____

_____

_____

_____

_____

_____

_____

_____

_____

_____

_____

Chapter 6

The Heart of a Fatherless Daughter

Dear God,

Dancing around in my pretty dress and showing off my new shoes I hope to hear him say I am beautiful, but instead there is silence. Does he not see me? Does he not hear me? "Daddy look at me," my heart says quietly. My cries go unheard as he goes about his day. Does he not know that I so desperately want to be daddy's girl? For so long I have cried from the memories of my daddy not seeing me. Yes, he was in my home, but he seemed to look through me and never really see me. I searched for so many years in so many men trying to find the love I did not get from him. God, why won't my daddy love me? Was I a bad little girl? I promise I will be good if he will just acknowledge me.   My heart is hungry for love from daddy.

The men I searched for love in had the same character as daddy, and they would not love me either. Was I not a good girl to them? I thought if I did all the right things that finally I could be enough. Again, I was wrong and only ended up having my heart torn into many pieces once more. I could feel myself shutting down.   I gave my body and not my heart in hopes one of them would say, "Baby Girl, I love you."

 As I sit before you, I want to know, "What did I do to daddy to turn him away from me?" I would wait for him to come home so I could sit on his lap and when I tried he pushed me away and told me he was tired. Could he not see he hurt my feelings and broke my heart? Time after time there was so much disappointment. God someone told me that you are my Father and my daddy. Is that true? If it is, will you turn away from me like my daddy? How can you love me when the man who helped to bring me into this world acts like I don't exist? Oh God, my heart is breaking in this moment as all the many years of pain come rushing back with the freshness of when it actually happened.

God for so long I said, "I do not care about daddy." Now I know that I care more that life itself. I have come to a place where my tears are constant companions. A daddy is supposed to love and cherish his daughter. He is supposed to tell her how pretty she is and let her know how loved she is. Well, I never had that. He never told me I was pretty, and I looked for boys and men to be a substitute for him. Yet, they never told me either. Am I ugly and that is why daddy would not say that I am pretty? As I have grown older I tell myself that if I wear enough makeup or comb my hair a certain way, that someone will tell me I am beautiful, but it does not happen. My tears have become the place where the little girl in me smothers her pain and heartbreak. I do not want anyone to know how much pain I am really in. I have begun to turn away or push away men and then I resent them for not doing for me what I need. When will this pain go away? How can I become what daddy wanted me to be so that I can hear him say, "I love you?" I will do anything God if you will just allow him to wrap his arms around me, acknowledge me and say, "I love you so much."

Daddy is dying now, and my time is running out but I still need him. When I am around him, the little girl within is front and center. She cries the tears of a toddler and the teenager who is still wondering what she has done for him to turn away. I am trembling, God, because I cannot let him go before he tells me what I have done wrong. Was I not his daughter? Was I too much like my mom? Did I not look the way he had hoped? Please, God, do not allow him to die without me having answers. My heart could never take it. God, if I allow you to hold my heart, will you take the pain away? It has become too much for me to carry. My heart is beating so strong and yet it is so weak. Daddy God, can I be your Baby Girl? I'm tired now. I do not know what else to do. Can I rest on your shoulder? Can I sit on your lap? Will you be my safe place of protection? I'm ready to allow you inside to unlock my hidden heart. I am afraid but somehow I believe I can trust you in ways I could not believe my father. I am ready God. I am resting my head on You, and I know my heart will never be the same.

Signed

A Fatherless Daughter

A daughter desires to be the apple of her father's eye. Even as a little girl she dances around the room and makes the prettiest little face in hopes that daddy will say, "Awe, look at my little angel, my princess." The sad fact is that many times daughters grow up hungering for what God says is rightfully theirs, the love of their fathers. In the limitations of a father's understanding of love, compassion and emotional commitment to his daughters, he sometimes, unknowingly, fails to give his daughter what she will desperately need as she becomes a young woman. As she grows into womanhood seeking and desiring the attention of young boys and men and then in her journey to discover her husband, what she did not receive from her father will be evident in her actions. Some fathers do not understand the importance of their relationships with their little girls. The wounds that are left behind because of the lack of love, affection, attention and correction given by a father to his daughter can have lasting effects upon her as a person and as a woman. There are times in her life that she seems to repeat the same cycles, yet she does not understand why.

A fatherless daughter does not mean that daddy is not there nor does it mean that daddy is deceased. The most tragic fatherless daughter relationship is the one whose father is physically present but absent in every other way. A father is to be the first man that a young girl loves. He is to be the first man who loves her. He is to show her how to be a lady and to be treated as such. He is to show her a man who is trustworthy and loyal towards her. He is to give her affirmations and hugs. He is to be that kind word. He is the first to tell her she is beautiful and smart. He is to correct and teach her. He is to tell her that she can do anything. He is to let her know that he has her back. Many times this does not happen, and the lack of those things not happening causes life altering wounds.

I remember in my life as a little girl I would wait for my daddy to come home so I could sit on his lap. I felt that my day was not complete without seeing him. Those moments when he rejected me from getting up into his lap because either he was too tired or he did not want to be bothered, wounded my heart and spirit each time it happened. I hoped he would be happy, just to see me. I simply wanted his attention. I wanted to bring a smile to his face. When the results I hoped for did not come, I was again wounded.

I began to seek out love and affection from boys and then men in hopes that it would replace the love, affection and attention that I had not received from daddy. I had cycles in my life with men who continued to break me down through their words and actions. After 20 years of marriage and forty plus years of life, I began to realize that I was searching for a love in others that could not replace my father's love that should have been rightfully mine. Unfortunately, my father did not know how to give what I needed from him. He was wounded himself, and he left me as a fatherless daughter.

Yet, God is saying…

You are my baby girl. Where your daddy was limited in his relationship with you, I Am your Father. Regardless of what your daddy chose not to give you, I Am your Father. Regardless of when your daddy abandoned you, I Am here for you. I feel your pain. I feel your desire to be loved. I know your heart is searching. I feel your hunger and thirst after love in other men, and I Am here to tell you that you know longer have to search, baby girl. I Am your daddy. I Am your Father. I will never leave you nor forsake you (Hebrews 13:5). You can trust in me. You can sit upon my lap as I hold you close and allow you to know that it is well. I will let you know that you are beautiful. I will hold you close and caress you, take away the longing and desire to seek the love of a father which you rightfully deserve, deliver you from the men who will continue to break you down. No longer do you need to be fatherless. No longer do you need to feel abandoned because I am here for you my daughter.

Your heart is hurting. Your heart is broken. Your heart is wounded and you have chosen to lock yourself away, even from me. My daughter I am telling you that I Am your Father, yet I know you question if I am the same as your earthly father. You are asking yourself if I am the same as the father who helped to give you life and yet abandoned you and turned his back on you. You saw him walk away, abuse your mother, be unfaithful in relationships and you wonder if I Am the same. No my child, I Am not him. I AM greater. I AM your first love. I Am the one who will heal you. Will you trust me? Will you allow me to be your father? Will you allow me into the hidden chambers of your heart where the love of a father should reside? Will you take my hand and walk with me? As you twirl in my presence and dance before me, you will bring joy to Me. You will bring a smile upon my heart. Will you allow Me to do the same to yours? I understand that it is not easy, but I want you to know I already know that you are wounded, and I will not turn away from you.

There is a place in your heart where I have not been allowed. You locked your daddy out and closed the area of your life and heart that was reserved for him because you did not want to be wounded again. If you will give me the key to the place in your heart where a father's love should be, I will come in and I will rest with you. From the father who walked away and never acknowledged you, I will take away the pain left behind. I will wipe away your tears and I will wipe away the illusion of love that you allowed men to give you in hoping they would replace your daddy's love.

I Am here for you, baby girl. Yes, your Father cares for you. I have always cared for you. I have watched you search high and low and embracing each time a man told you that you were beautiful because you were so needy of it. I have watched you each time a man made you smile because of the words he spoke, yet his actions were deceptive and left you increasingly broken. Each time those situations happened, the lock to your heart became stronger. Yet, I see you now becoming hard because you have made yourself bound to your pain. You have made the lock so strong that it will take a powerful Love to even attempt to release you from the pain of your past. Your father gave you what only he could give you, and yes, it left you wounded, but do you know that he was also wounded? Yes your daddy was supposed to love you. However, if he was not given what he needed himself, he does not know how to give it to you. Sometimes you hoped your daddy would desire to learn. You must understand that he did not know how to desire to know more or do better. He did not know how to look within himself to see his limitations or to hear your pain. He did what he could. Now allow Me to do the rest for you. You do not have to look for love within others.

Are you ready to open the door and let down the walls? You can take Me at My Word and you will never be forsaken again. Baby Girl, your Father is here who will dance with you, hold you, and allow you to cry. I will take away the mask of strength and show you your beauty for your ashes. Are you ready, are you ready, and are you ready? It is your time. It is time. Let's walk together and unlock the chains that have kept you bound so that you can receive the love of a Father and no longer be Fatherless.

Scriptures for a Fatherless Daughter-Comfort:

Psalm 9:9

9: The Lord also will be a refuge for the oppressed. A refuge in times of trouble

Psalm 9:10

10: And those who know Your name will put their trust in You; For You, Lord, have not forsaken those who seek you

Psalm 68:5 A father to the fatherless, and a judge of the widows, is God in His holy habitation.

Psalm 138:3

3: In the day when I cried out, You answered me, And made me bold with strength in my soul

Isaiah 58:11

11: The Lord will guide you continually, and satisfy your soul in drought, and strengthen your bones; You shall be like a watered garden, and like a spring of water, whose waters do not fail

Proverbs 16:9

9: A man's heart plans his way But The Lord directs his steps

Reflection:

_____

_____

_____

_____

_____

_____

_____

_____

_____

_____

_____

_____

_____

_____

_____

Chapter 7

A Mother's Broken Heart

Dear God,

In this moment I am numb. Emotionally I am drained. I am quiet and I dare not speak a word. Silence is working for me right now for some reason. I have not said a word for the past hour. The events of the day have caused me to shut down. My heart is sitting in my chest beating, but I do not even know what I am feeling right now.

I am a mom. I have lived my life since becoming a mom for my children. I have done everything within my power to be a good mom, to love them unconditionally and show them that I have their back. God why am I here again with a broken heart because of my child? How could they betray me over and over again? Where did I fail? What did I do, God? My heart is trying to shut down on me. I can feel it. I do not know if I will ever be able to trust him again. I do not know if I can allow him into the same place within my heart where I carried him daily. It hurts so much, Jesus. Satan uses my children to hurt me because he knows they mean the world to me. Oh, God my heart. How much more can it take and still beat. Please, God, help me so that I do not shut down and shut him out. My heart God is shattered. I cannot look at him without being more hurt than angry.

My trust in them has been broken and destroyed. Why, God, do I have to always be hurt? My heart feels so fragile right now. God, please take away the pain. I feel like a wounded bird. All that I have done for my children is for nothing. Again, Lord, I desperately ask You, what did I do? The betrayal, the lying and the deception is too much. How can those whom I carried within my womb be the source of my torment? Jesus, it hurts so much. Can they not see how they take my heart and rip it into pieces? Jesus, I need you in this moment.

Without you I will surely lock myself away within myself. Even though I know the devil seeks to destroy me and he is using my children, I still see my childs' face breaking me into shattered pieces. How do I get from this moment to loving them without reserve as I once did? How do I trust them and forgive them again? Does my heart not matter? I don't know where I go from this moment.

Signed

A Broken Hearted Mother

When a mother loves her children and seeks to give them all of her to ensure they know they are loved, protected and she has their back, it is painful when in turn she is broken by the same children. It is painful and life crushing trying to understand how the one's she gives life to take away life from her. Each time they lie to her, betray her, and stab the knife in her back with great force, the relationship is on the verge of collapsing.

As a mother you want to build a trusting relationship with your child. In the moment you discover that the child you thought you knew has been deceiving you for a long time, it can cause a pain so deep. It causes you to go into the vault of your heart. It pushes you to lock yourself away in order for the hurt to not be felt. In these moments, mothers can question God wandering what she may or may not have done to cause this. She sits still in too much pain to feel and too stunned to speak. It becomes a pain that no mother ever wants to feel. It is a battle within not to shut her children out of her heart. How can she do that when she loves them so? In the same breath she cries out to God in desperation and even in fear that she can never trust her child again with the innocence she once did.

The chamber of her heart seems to clang shut with such a force that stills her in her tracks. She struggles to see them as young adults and not her babies. Yet, when the pain comes from them, it reminds her that satan will use whomever is open to him, even her babies. The innocence in their eyes is gone. The truth in their words will always be questioned after the betrayal. She can feel herself going within behind her hearts secret chamber. She does not want to believe that her precious baby can hurt her in such a shattering way. Can she love again? Can she come out of her wall of defense and allow them to reside in the place of her heart only purposed for them? The door wants to be sealed as she feels herself going deeper into hiding. Will she be free to continue to love them or fear the pain happening again?

I wrote this message on my Restore Her Worth Business page in hopes that the broken hearted would be encouraged: "A Broken Heart is the reflection of someone who tried, gave and lived. It is not a death sentence even though it feels that way. It is a momentary injury that can be the birth place of purpose, strength and elevation. It's not over until God says it is. It is in the broken places that His strength is made PERFECT. I believe a woman's heart can take much and bounce back. Yet, to have heartbreak from a child is greater than the abandonment of a parent or the lack of love from a parent. A mother gives her children all of her in hopes that they will respect and love her enough to see all that she has done and sacrificed for them and be one of the people who protects her heart. Sometimes a child does not understand the pain they can cause a parent until they are older. This does not negate the fact that there has been pain. Sometimes the pain is never let go, and the relationships between mom and child can be destroyed. Yet, I believe if she is able to allow God to enter into that sensitive space of her heart and trust Him with the anger, betrayal, and unforgiveness toward her child, she can be stronger than ever before.

In her moment of brokenness she freezes unable to breath and yet she hears God say to her.......

My daughter, O my daughter, cry no more. Trust me in this pain as you have trusted me in all others. I hear the doors shutting and the key being turned to lock yourself away. I know you see your children as the source of your pain. Yes, satan is using them to penetrate the part of you that I desire to use but you only see their faces. Remember who your enemy really is. It is the one who is the betrayer. It is the one who deceives. It is the one who comes to sift you. It is satan himself. You may not understand this right now, but I will take all that you are feeling in this moment and use it for your good. I will take it all and use it for My Glory. Your heart for your children has always been to give them all of you, even when you were shattered into so many pieces. You wanted them to never feel abandoned or unwanted. Don't shut yourself away again. Satan wants you to turn your back on them and your relationship with them. Your love for them is too deep for that. If you will trust me, I will teach you to protect your heart with My Word and still love fully.

It will not be easy, yet in order for you to walk into the purpose I have called you to, you must give Me this burden and your relationship with them. Yes, give it to Me. Give them to Me, and in turn they will stand before you and bless you. Can you trust Me? Can you give me your mother's heart for them? You are a mother and your love for them runs deep like a river. Your love for them is deeper than the Red Sea. Allow me to take the pain of the betrayal and devour it in the Sea of Forgetfulness where you will never see it again. It is easier for you to lock your heart and try to not feel. It is easier for you to grow angry with them. This time please trust Me. Allow me to come into your secret chamber where the love for your children resides. The key is safe with me. I will not let your love for them destroy you. I will build you. I will refresh you. I will teach you to love them through my heart for you. Allow me to parent you right now in your unrest and brokenness from the betrayal your heart is receiving. One day they will respect your love for them, and you will be able to believe their words when they say they love you. I Am here to wipe your tears and cleanse you. Are you ready? Are you ready? Are you really ready to allow Me inside the safe place you run to when again your trust and heart are broken? You can trust me with the key and my loyalty is true to you. I am your Father and I Am here for you now. Rest your mother muscles in my strength and allow me to be the breasted One for you. This too shall pass in that you can be assured and now you can rest in Me.

Scriptures for Broken Hearted Daughter/Mother-Comfort:

Psalm 141:1

1: Lord, I cry out to You; Make hast to me! Give ear to my voice when I cry out to you

Psalm 141:8

8: But my eyes are upon you, O God The Lord; in You I take refuge; Do not leave my soul destitute

Psalm 141: 3

3: Set a guard, O Lord over my mouth; Keep watch over the door of my lips

James 3:17

17: But the wisdom that is from above is first pure, then peaceable, gentle, willing to yield, full of mercy and good fruits, without partiality and without hypocrisy.

2 Thessalonians 2:16

16: Now may our Lord Jesus Christ Himself, and our God and Father, who has loved us and given us everlasting consolation and good hope by grace

Reflection:

Chapter 8

A Suicidal Heart

Dear God,

How did I get to this place? I feel so heavy. The pain is so deep it is penetrating my soul. It is cutting every place it touches like a razor blade. Why God? Why so much hurt? Today all the hurt, betrayal, loneliness, abandonment, fear and more seems to be attacking me along with the pain of today. I cannot take anymore. I do not want to live if all I will feel is pain. Why won't they love me and treat me right? I gave them my love. I gave them my heart. I gave them my body. I was honest and trusting. In return they lied, manipulated, cheated and misused me. Why? Lord, don't they see how much I love them? Why am I not enough? I can't take this anymore. This thing called life is too much. I just want to sleep. Maybe if I sleep and don't wake up they would care and see how much their actions hurt someone else.

Sleep, a deep sleep, will stop me from feeling these forty plus years of pain. I won't be a burden anymore to others. No one understands how deeply I have hurt daily. I have these Xanax here, and they normally help me to sleep when just taking one. If I take multiple, I will get a good, deep sleep right? Then the pain will end and I can rest. God I am screaming inside. Do you hear me? Do you feel this earth shattering pain within me?

I sent the goodbye text to all those I love except my children. I do not want them to know. They will simply believe that I am taking a long sleep. God I hear this voice in my head telling me every time someone has made my heart hurt, that I deserved it. The voice is telling me my daddy did not love me and men won't either because I am not good enough.

I thought to myself, "So many pills in my hand," I should just let go. Am I really going to do this? I am so scared, God. I took one and swallowed it. The others will be easy also because they are so small. I can take them all at once. This feeling of hopelessness is getting stronger. This time satan means to take me out. I feel overwhelmed of all the thoughts beating me down within. The phone is ringing. My loved ones have received my goodbye texts. I do not want to talk. I just want to sleep. All I want to do is rest. I do not want to die. I just want the pain to stop and go away. I am tired of hurting. God I feel the first pill starting to take effect. I am leaning into my hands with my mouth covering all the other pills. As the devil tells me to "go ahead and do it," I find my last bit of strength to say, "God help me."

It is morning and I am still here. Why am I awake? I see the pills in my bed, so I know I did not take all of them. The pain is so intense. My heart feels broken and shattered into bits and pieces. My family is calling. I am groggy. I look at the phone and say, "please leave me alone." When I finally answer the phone, I hear my brother's voice on the phone asking me, "What did you do, sis?" I cannot tell him because I am so groggy. I told him

I just want to sleep. God does he even realize that all I feel is despair, pain and death inside me. I do not hear his words. They are not penetrating the pain.

Dear God, if you want me, I am ready. God help me please...

If you can take the pain, please do. I am begging you to stop the hurt. I do not want to die. My children need me, but I cannot live anymore like this...

Signed,

A Suicidal Daughter

Suicide has become an epidemic. From the youngest to the oldest, many have come to the place where they feel the pain they are feeling is too hard to bare any longer. They believe the only thing left to do is to leave this world as they know it.

This feeling is far too familiar to me. In 2013, I was at the point of feeling I could not take another heartache. I could not take any more abandonment. I could not take anything less than love for another second. From what I have seen, heard and read, many times as Christians we are judgmental towards those who have attempted suicide or completed the act of taking their life. Some think the person was weak. Some believe people are not strong enough or just did not trust or believe in God enough. Some even believe that a person is selfish when they attempt or complete the act of suicide. Many times this is far from the truth.

I pray for anyone reading these words that you never reach the point of your pain being so unbearable that you feel the only way to live is to die. This is a pain and a place where no one should ever have to be, yet it happens daily. Not being able to withstand any more pain does not say that we do not trust or believe God. It does not mean that someone is being selfish. Sometimes it is a cry for help to say, "Please see me." It is asking the question, "Can you please stop hurting me?" and "Don't you see that I am beaten down enough?" There are moments that we can cry out in despair hoping someone will answer the call and rescue us.

In 2013, I had come to a place in my life where all the pain from childhood and adulthood had accumulated into one moment and one season. I was in a place where I felt if I continued to live, life would be a continuation of the same pain until I took my last breath. In those moments, it was not that I wanted to die, I simply wanted to sleep. Somehow I had taught myself over the years that when I slept I did not feel, hurt, or think. I wanted to have a deep sleep because the pain cut to the core of my being. It was as if the last brick in my coffin had been placed on me.

When your heart has been ripped into pieces so many times, it becomes a feeling that it can never be repaired. You can come to an understanding that it hurts too much to live. You do not necessarily want to leave your family behind. You surely do not want other people to hurt that you leave to morn for you. In those moments your pain is in complete control for the first time. Someone else has always been in control of the pain brought upon you. In those moments of life and death you believe this is your way of taking back your control for yourself.

As I lie in bed looking into my hand filled with Xanax, I knew within myself I did not want to die, but I did not want to feel anymore. I just wanted to sleep. It really hurts me when I see other Christian's judge and condemn someone who has committed suicide or attempted to commit suicide. It breaks my heart because they do not realize the blessing they have in never experiencing this type of pain. In the early morning hours of despair, it was never that I did not love God or did not know or believe He loves me. In fact I knew without a doubt that God loves me. In my human state I was under a place where I felt suffocated. When you say, "If one more thing happens, I will not be able to take it" and the one thing happens, it can be a death sentence in your own heart and mind.

It was not about who was in my life at the time or what they had done. In my mind and spirit it was an addition to all the others who had done the same exact thing. It was not about the person in my life, although they would like to think they are the reason I was at my low point. It was a continuation of a lifetime of rejection and feeling unloved, unworthy, and of feeling as if I did not matter to anyone. It was a repeat of the words replaying in my head that told me, "nobody wants you, nobody cares if you live or die, or no one will pay attention if you are not here." As I lied in bed I remembered being a child, saying when I would say the right thing or doing the right action to give others the impression that I may kill myself in order for them to acknowledge me or pay attention to me.

As you read these words you may think, "Did she really say that?" Yes, I pretended. I am not afraid to be vulnerable before you. As long as we stay hidden we remain broken. As I always say, "What is hidden cannot be healed." I pray in my vulnerability and transparency that it will help someone else. Even as a child I felt unwanted, unloved and unseen. Pretending I would hurt myself was my cry for help that went unanswered. I am thankful that even then God was protecting me from satan's tactics to steal my life. In those moments in 2013, there was no pretending. There was no trying to get attention, no cry out for other people's attention in my lowest moment. The feelings were real. My decision was real. I was at the point of ending it all, and it was not for show. Somehow before I put one Xanax in my mouth, I found the strength to say, "God help me." I believe it was that simple prayer that saved my life. I took one Xanax and slept until the next morning. As I woke, I could see all the pills that were in my hand had fallen into the bed around me. Realizing I was still alive angered me. The events that finally got me to my feet that day feel like a dream. It was not an easy twelve or more hours but God brought me through it. I realized that I was meant to live and I chose to live one moment at a time.

I remember when my brother called the person who was in my life at the time and told him what was going on, he called and really acted like it was inconvenience to him to be bothered with my issues. My brother reached out to him and told him to "leave me alone if he was not going to treat me right." I recalled when I saw this person weeks later, they said to me, 'you tried to kill yourself...that is the craziest thing I have ever heard." I am so thankful that God had strengthened me and sustained me for that moment. Unfortunately, he came to the conclusion that it was about him, which is a sad point. However; he was indeed the person satan used to apply the final brick. The matter was never about him, but the spiritual battle that was against me. He was just the physical representation of the battle. His words made me numb. Yet, I was also feeling strong and knew that his words or the words that satan gave him, no longer controlled me and I could walk away and live.

A heart that is burdened and buried under the weight of everything that tells it that it is hated or unwanted, sometimes cannot find a shovel strong enough to remove the strength of the lies that the devil has told it. Therefore, the heart decides to stop fighting, give in and agree with what it hears and feels and allow the lies to take over. A suicidal heart comes to a place where it releases what it knows to be true and simply chooses to let go of it all. Our heart can carry heavy weight and still live and beat. It doesn't change the truth that sometimes in those moments of despair it feels that my heart, your heart, cannot take another morsel of what seems to be a continuous cycle in our lives.

As I was able to find the courage, with Gods' help, to get back up, so can you. God sent my child to me, and I did not know he was aware of what was going on. My brother had called him to give me an antidote because he wasn't sure if I had taken the pills or not due to me being so groggy on the phone. To see the pain in my child's' eyes when he asked me, "mama did you take all those pills?" I could not get up for myself. Yet, with Gods' help I chose to get up for my son, for my children. Eventually I was able to get up for myself also. My love for my children is such that I never intentionally want to hurt them. In a flash I saw the trauma and the chaos that would occur in their lives if I was not alive. In that moment, their pain was more than I could bear. Their pain was more important to me than my own pain.

God is saying to you:

To My daughter reading these words believing that no one cares about you, that no one will miss you, and no one wants you around, this is not true. You, the one who needs someone to say, "I see your pain." Well, I say to you, I not only see your pain, but I feel your pain, and I hear your pain. I know what you are in need of. I will bring people into your life who will help you through these moments. I have counselors and others who will listen without judgment and give you a safe place to open your heart. I will bring those into your life that I have purposely connected to you to help you find your confidence, your strength and your hope. My daughter, I have heard your cries in the midnight hours. I have felt the stabbing pain as words were spoken that touched those wounded places in your heart cutting you like a sword. As you allow others to help you, just know that it is not a sign of weakness. In fact, it shows the inner strength that you already have as you are reaching for help. You no longer have to live in this bondage or silence alone. No matter how you came to this cave of darkness and despair in your life, no matter where you go, I Am there. When there was no one else around you, I was there.

Satan was there also telling you to take every pill and telling you that no one will ever love you or care for you. As satan lied to you and laughed at you, you chose to reach out to Me. As you choose to answer the call of life, you shall live. I Am leading you to trustworthy people whose hearts I have touched to receive you. It is time for you to give the keys to the cave within your heart to me. It has become too much for you. Will you believe Me? Will you trust Me? I heard you as the thoughts of suicide judged you and weighted you down. Yet, know that it will not always be this way. It is time for you to rise up out of the ashes and live. My daughter I Am here and I will never leave you (Hebrews 13:5). Your heart and pain is safe with me. It is time for you to heal and face your hidden pain and shame so that you can rise up. As you rise up from the ashes, you are becoming the woman that I birthed you to be before the beginning of time. Your life is valuable. You are valuable. Others' lives will truly be affected if you are not here. I gave you purpose. If there was not a need for you to be here, you would not have been conceived in your mother's womb. You are important. You are priceless. The people who have caused you the pain you are feeling right now don't realize it's not about them. It is about the woman that I have purposed you to be. Satan knows if you deal with the garbage that is inside of you that is holding you back, you come into your own, own your truth and stand in your power that you are a force to be reckoned with.

So my daughter, I call to your heart. I call to your spirit and your mind. Turn the keys over to me. Allow me to come in and be everything that you need, want and desire to be whole.

Are you ready? Are you ready my daughter? It is your time. Come out of the cave and walk with me...

Scriptures for a Suicidal Heart-Comfort:

Ecclesiastes 7:17

17: Do not be overly wicked, nor be foolish: Why should you die before your time?

Psalm 34:17

17: The righteous cry out and The Lord hears, and delivers them out of all their troubles

Psalm 34:18

18: The Lord is near to those who have a broken heart and saves such as have a contrite spirit

Psalm 34:19

19: Many are the afflictions of the righteous, but the Lord delivers him out of them all

Psalm 34: 22

22: The Lord redeems the soul of His servants, and none of those who trust in Him shall be condemned

Reflection:

_____

_____

_____

_____

_____

_____

_____

_____

_____

_____

_____

_____

_____

_____

_____

Chapter 9

A Heart of Insignificance

Dear God,

This is not easy for me to say, but I'm supposed to be honest with you, right? Well, I'm not sure how to do that when I am afraid to be honest with myself. It is too painful to admit that I do not feel worthy. There I said it. I still do not feel any better by admitting it. I guess that is why I always get hurt because I feel I am not worthy of any better. It is almost as if I am waiting for rejection or denial. I do not know how to expect anything else. The funny thing is when the rejection and denial come, it is a self-proclaimed prophesy, and I still fall apart under the weight of it. I want happiness but I prepare myself for sadness. I want love, but I prepare myself for their infidelity, lies or abandonment. I see love, happiness, self-fulfillment, exciting careers, family joy, and I want it all like a child wants a bag full of candy. Somehow in the same breath I believe that there is something that I have done that makes it impossible to have all of this for myself.

I remember as a child when I would sing, I was never chosen to lead solos at school. There were always the same 2 or 3 people who were chosen instead of me. Each time this happened, I became even quieter within myself. I figured if I was good enough, I would have been chosen. After a while I accepted that I was not good enough because if I were then I would have been standing in front of our auditorium singing my heart out. I could feel myself hiding within hoping no one would see the pain I felt with each rejection or denial. I realize now that I was expecting it to come even then.

I hear other people tell me I am worthy of love, I am worthy to be loved, I am worthy to succeed, and I am worthy to do what I want to do in life. Do they not realize that I'm not listening, and I do not believe them? God it hurts so badly when they say this to me. It hurts mostly because I feel that they have a hope and expectation in me that I cannot possibly complete.

I feel like a failure.

Okay, God, I am ready to speak the truth completely. When I was a little girl, my daddy was always gone. My mom was really angry all the time. When daddy came home, I was always happy to see him. Yet, it always seemed to turn into a war zone between my parents. What I hoped and wanted to be a happy time was the total opposite. There was so much anger and loud talking that I wished I could stuff cotton so far into my ears that I did not hear a sound. I wanted to hear the sound that I saw on television. You know--the sound of laughter, the parents getting along and the children jumping and playing with daddy as he came in from work every day. I felt, as the oldest, that I could make it better but I only made it worse. When daddy would stay gone for days at time, I felt that if I had been better that he

would have come home. I thought it was my fault.
I felt if I cleaned up better, my mom would not be
angry. It seemed that I lived within a war zone
and I lived on the edge.

Somehow I took all this as me not being good
enough. If I was enough, daddy would be happy
when he came home because I was showing him
how happy I was to see him. I tried to love on him
as best I could as a child but he was usually too
tired or did not want to be bothered.

As an adult I feel like I am invisible to the world
around me. I do not matter to anyone. I am not
important to anyone. Was I not enough? Am I not
good enough for others to acknowledge me? Was
I wrong to want my daddy's attention? I have
always felt when I open my mouth to speak, that
nothing comes out. It seems to me others tune me
out when I speak, or they hear me talking but they
are not listening, at least it's how I see it. This
world feels so empty even though there are
millions of people around me. I am a voice that is

not heard, as a child and even now as an adult, I am not heard.

I just do not matter.

Signed an Insignificant Heart

The feeling of being insignificant can be overwhelming. It is the feeling of living and breathing and seeing everyone else around you as giants and yourself as a meager mouse trying to climb the ladder to be as big as everyone else. Yet, in all your struggles to climb the ladder you still feel insignificant and unimportant to all the people who actually take a moment to look upon your face. There is the moment of asking yourself, "Why don't I matter, Why am I never good enough, Why don't I feel as important as the other people whom I see?"

It is easy to think that feeling insignificant, feeling as if you do not matter or feeling that you are not important begins in your adulthood. However, in many things and most likely in all things that we struggle within our lives, the struggle begins when we are much younger. In my life, at least, this is the case.

In my childhood there was this one word that I was called over and over again that I didn't realize the impact it would have in my life even as a 40 eight year old woman. I could see great things happening to other people but somewhere deep inside I felt that I was not valuable or important enough to have those same things or even more to happen to me. This one little word, these few little letters of the alphabet were powerful. When this word was spoken to me it caused me to feel like the measly mouse walking close to the ground and unable to climb beyond the two inch little legs that carried me. The word is "Trifling." This word was said to me in anger. This word said to me that I was nothing.

When I would hear this word being said to me, I somehow assumed it was something to do with my body and/or sex. As a child, when I would hear this word being yelled at me, in my mind I felt like I was being called a whore or trashy. It made me feel I was someone who gave their body away to boys and did not care about the importance of who she was. I felt that I was told I only wanted and was interested in being with boys. I felt nasty and put down each time it was spoken. I was none of the things that this word made me feel. Each time I heard it something in me died.

I lived with the belief and the lie of what this word meant for many years. In fact all the way into my adult years I really believed I was being called a whore and trashy. However, it would be many years later before understanding just what I was being called. According to the Oxford Online Dictionary, trifling: means unimportant and insignificant. When I realize the true meaning of trifling, the light bulbs inside of me brightened. The bells began to ring and suddenly it was clear to me. What I felt in my life, how I saw myself was a direct reflection of a word. That small word with the few letters of the alphabet that had replayed over and over again, in my spirit, my mind and mostly in my heart had become as a giant to me. Even though the word was no longer being said to me, the feelings, my vision of myself, my lack of belief in myself, how I saw myself in the eyes of others had been developed by and through the word trifling.

I believe in our lives that God knows, decides and releases the answers to the many questions we have about why we constantly struggle with certain things. He knows the time when we will be able to hear and accept the answers. As I look back at the moment when God allowed me to hear and receive what trifling means, I now understand I would not have been ready to receive the truth, had the answer come sooner. I would have made an excuse for it or even more, denied it altogether. When God released the answer to this one thing that had tormented me all my life, I was in a place where I desired healing and truth. I wanted to be more than what I had been. God was already showing me I was more than I had believed. I could see God moving me into a new realm of how I see myself, how I believe in myself and how I visualize the way He sees me. We spend so much time wondering how other people see us until we lose sight of how we should see ourselves. We also lose sight of what is most important, how God already sees us.

Because I felt insignificant, I closed the part of my heart to the world and to God that would say to me that I was loved and good enough. I felt if others saw this part of me they would continue to show me that I did not matter. The thought of this happening was too painful. Somehow, I came to the conclusion, if I showed God my broken places and spoke of my mistakes to Him, He would also show me I did not matter. Thankfully this is not the truth.

I did not realize I had shut myself down because of what I felt about myself. I always expected to be treated the way I felt about myself. I expected it to happen, even if it was not the reality. In fact, I really believe that I self-sabotaged myself by believing and accepting that my life would always be this way.

We can walk through life as wounded soldiers until we decide to allow the physician, the Great Physician, Jesus Christ to come within the private places of our heart. The part of our heart that has been bolted down so no one gains entry holds the secrets to our pain and will give us the answers we need to not only live, but thrive. As we begin to trust Jesus with the full access of who we are, the dry places within us begin to hunger and thirst for living water.

As God revealed the truth of why I felt insignificant, the well within me was dry and thirsting. The place where God was bringing me was a place where I was near the water but because I had locked away the parts of me that could feel, I had to give God access. I needed to give God permission to not just stand at the door of my heart, but to give Him entry. This room within my own heart was not even acknowledged by me because it was too dark to enter.

We have locked ourselves away for far too long. Sometimes we believe if we do not matter then why bother allowing someone inside who could really love us. Especially when our past has shown that we only know how to allow those within who say they love us, yet in fact they do not. When we believe we do not matter, we will take whatever we get and however it seems to come.

But God is saying to us:

My daughter...

The words that have been spoken over you, the treatment you have received does not define your value. You have mattered to Me always. You mattered to Me as I formed every part of you. Every cell and every hair on your head, I created in you. Do you believe I would take the time and create something as beautiful and unique as you, if you did not matter?

You have been told things in your childhood that even now as a woman you struggle with. You struggle to find something different and greater because of what you have always known. Did you know that all those things built you into this moment? Yes, you were tested and tried by the words that were spoken. You were tested and beaten down with words by the people who came into your life who continued to pour into you what you already felt about yourself. Yet My daughter, it never changed how I see you. It never changed who I know you to be. The ones who wounded you, were wounded themselves. They spoke to you out of anger because they did not know how to express any other emotion. In their anger, they wounded you, and in return you saw yourself as a mouse when you are so much more. Now, I need you to look up from the position of a mouse and see yourself bigger, stronger, wiser, and braver and more than all the words that are piled upon you from childhood until now. It is time for you to raise your back and your head and see your legs stronger and longer than the two inches that you have believed you walked on. Begin to see your back strong enough to carry the woman you are today. I Am calling you out of insignificance because I have birthed great purpose in you. You do not have permission to shrink. You do not have permission to live life any less that what I created in you. I have called you for such a time as this. It is time for you to see yourself upon the mountain top and crossing the red sea. It is time for the word trifling to release you and let you go.

You are My daughter. I AM your Father. Will you trust Me with the part of your heart where I can show you how much you matter? It does not matter what you have heard before this moment. It is now that I ask You to hear and receive My Word as it is life for you. I have always loved you. Nothing can separate you from Me. You are valuable to Me. The words that were spoken over your life as of this moment will no longer have power over you. You shall live life abundantly from this moment forward. As you stand in your own power, raise your head and push your shoulders back, now you are no longer in the position of a mouse. You stand in a position of power because you are a woman of significance. We will walk through this door together as you discover who you are. You will give birth to your purpose and together you will walk into the woman that I created you to be. She has always been inside of you. When you found the courage to desire her and go in search of more than you have known, you made the choice to accept what they called you, but to no longer allow it to define you. You chose to believe that you are more. Take my hands and let's walk to together. It is time for you to be free.......

Scriptures for Feeling Unworthy-Comfort:

1 Corinthians 6:20

20: For you were brought at a price; therefore glorify God in your body and in the spirit, which are God's

Matthew 10:29

29: Are not two sparrows sold for a copper coin? And not one of them falls to the ground apart from your Father's will

Isaiah 43:4

4: Since you were precious in my sight, You have been honored, and I have loved you; Therefore I will give men for you, and people for your life

Jeremiah 29:11

11: For I know the thoughts that I think toward
you, says The Lord, thoughts of peace and not of
evil, to give you a future and a hope

John 6:37

37: All that The Father gives Me will come to Me,
and the one who comes to Me I will by no means
cast out

Reflection:

_____

_____

_____

_____

_____

_____

_____

_____

_____

_____

_____

_____

_____

_____

Chapter 10

You Can Breathe Now Baby Girl

God knows that our desire was not to feel the pain, go through the betrayal and distrust or face the scars that we carried within. However; He is always waiting patiently for you to invite Him to begin the healing process. You no longer have to carry around the burden of the keys that kept you bound. Those keys hindered the blood flow of the spirit of God from dwelling in the secret place. You have been delivered and your wounds are covered in the blood of Jesus.

When the natural heart becomes dysfunctional an assessment must be done in order to find the source of the blockage. The clots in the blood stream must be destroyed in order for the blood to reach every part of the heart unit. Our heart has been clogged for far too long with the matters of the heart. God has come as you have trusted Him with the deteriorating parts of you and now your blood flow is reaching the vital parts of you: your mind, your spirit, your purpose and your heart now beats with a new beat.

You are a warrior. Warriors know when there needs to be a compromise and when there needs to be a fight. As you have trusted God, you chose to yield to His Grace, Truth and Love. You chose not to fight against Him and instead you allowed your walls to fall. Your willingness to trust in the place where you were betrayed is being filled with gratefulness. Your walls know longer are needed against Him and He has come in to allow you to rest in Him.

The little girl in you can be free so the woman in the mirror can breathe. The little girl looking for daddy's love has found the arms of her Father. She can sit on her Father's lap as He calls to her and she knows she is safe. She recognizes that He is like no other and she no longer has to protect herself from Him but instead allow herself to be totally vulnerable before Him without judgment or shame. She is ready to run through the fields of her life as light as a feather because her weights have been lifted. You are the woman that carried the baggage of the little girl within at the point of her pain and the woman trying to live beyond it. There is no more separation between the two of you. You are now one.

The Father has been received into the secret chamber and all the secrets are revealed. The division or the blockage has been found and the love of God has applied the medication needed to allow the flow of healing to take place.

In all your unwritten letters to God, He heard you. He felt your heartache. He waited for you. He waited for His daughter to give over her letters of pain in exchange for healing. Your words were heard through your tears when they filled your pillow.

Your letters are now changed from pain to powerful. You can exhale as the clots in the arteries of your inner court have been expelled. You can breathe and thrive as your lungs breathe in a new sense of life never before experience in your life.

I can hear the doors swinging within as the love of God touches each one and they freely open. Everything behind them no longer has a place to hide. You journey has not been easy. Your choice to give God the keys that you believed you needed to hold on to in order to convince yourself that you were in control, is a powerful one. It has not been easy to let go. Yet, it is letting go that allowed you to step into the woman you were created to be.

Each day we choose to release, forgive, understand and own our truth in our story, we take back the parts of our life that pain took away. I applaud you in this moment. I celebrate with you. I see you. I hear you. You are a giant standing tall in your own power and strength.

I am my sister. My sister is me.

This is a defining moment for the remainder of our lives. As the old gatekeeper of our heart tries to return to take ownership of the rooms within us, we are reminded that the enemy was devoured in the Red Sea as he tried to overtake Gods people. We are Gods' daughters and He covers us. The journey you have decided to take with me, know that you are not alone.

It is time for the daughters of God to rise up out of the ashes of pain, shame and silence. It is time for the daughters of God to step into the sunshine. That means it is your time. Yes, you. No matter the size of your body, the length of your hair, how attractive you are or how educated you are, you simply matter.

Gods' loving hands are holding yours. It is a moment of transformation in our lives to be able to see ourselves as the one who can speak on top of the well instead of being stuck deep down within in. God has taken every tear and every wound and allowed His loving touch to heal it from the inside out. Our wounds no longer have to ooze under the doors of the locked chambers that we call our heart.

Breathe, Baby Girl. Our King has come and all the doors are forever open so you can face what is there and allow God to walk with you through the stages of breakthrough. This is the beginning and the end of the hiding. What remains in between is a place of growth. As you begin your new journey, wear your crown of grace proudly.

Breathe, Baby Girl. Our Father has placed us on His lap, and we are fulfilled. No longer are we searching for daddy's love or mamma's approval. We are no longer living as mice. We are no longer seeing other people as the only ones who are able to live life to the fullest. We have inhaled pain and exhaled healing. We inhaled less than and exhaled more than enough through the exchange of what was for what is. Now is our moment. Now the ashes have released us and beauty has arrived.

Come into the light, Baby Girl. All that the world holds, awaits you. Your tears may come, but now you know they are cleansing you and building you. As the light shines upon your face, throw your head back and walk in the fullness of all it beholds just for you.

Your sisters need you. You need your sisters. As the barriers that held you at bay with each other are torn down, each of you are open to receive one another. We need each other to stop, look and listen to our heartbeat. With each heartbeat we give each other the medication God allows to flow through each of us to heal, restore and Thrive.

Breathe, Baby Girl...It is time to for you to Soar. Your wings are spread wide and they are no longer broken.......Go in peace.

Reflection:

_____

_____

_____

_____

_____

_____

_____

_____

_____

_____

_____

_____

_____

_____

Chapter 11

Final Thoughts

Dear Sister Friend

I am so thankful you have allowed me to pour out my heart to you. I pray that as I have laid my pain before you, you realize you are not alone. My desire is for you to see yourself in my pain and find the courage to uncover your own. I know this journey is not easy. As I walk and live my own life journey, I have come to understand that I am forever evolving.

Your journey is your own. There is power in your journey. In this moment you may feel that the pain will never go away. You may feel a sense of hopelessness because you have dealt with some things all your life. Just know there is hope before you. There is a moment in all our lives when we begin to accept that we deserve to be happy. Choosing to be happy will require a willingness to face what has held our happiness back. It all begins within.

No matter what has occurred in your life that caused you to shut down and walk away from who you are, never forget that your happiness is for you. Your pain has a purpose. Yes, my sister, there is a purpose in everything you have faced. You are here for a purpose.

In the past, I never thought I was valuable, so I never believed I could be more than the girl who was cheated on. I never thought I would be more than the one who was always left behind. To believe that I could feel love from God, others and towards myself, was a fairytale.

Yet, here I am sharing my hearts pain with the world that I might help other women maneuver their own hurt. When we allow ourselves to be vessels of healing, then the pain, and all of its power, is not in vain. You, my sister, will live out your fairytale as well. I believe in you. More than my belief in you, God has always believed in you. You matter to Him. He loves you so much. He knows your beginning and end. He also knows where you are in this moment. You have not been forgotten. You matter. You matter to me. If you were not here, so many people's lives would not be the same. Please tell yourself right this moment: I AM VALUABLE AND I MATTER. I know it may not be easy to say it right now as it was not for me either. However; today I can say it BOLDLY. Your day will come also, and if it already has, I APPLAUDE YOU.

Your journey to open your heart will require vulnerability. In my first book, "*The Journey to Uncover The Real Me: Finding Myself Through God's Love*," I discovered that I cannot hold back what I considered my private business. The beauty of God healing and delivering us is the freedom received is not only for us, but the ones He has divinely connected to us. I would not be able to write these words to you had I not given up my right to care about what others would say when they read my story. My story has birthed my purpose. My purpose is to meet other woman and girls where I have been and show them through my pain, healing and deliverance that there is greater and better for their lives.

I am proud of you for reading this evolution of my heart and healing. Again, I applaud you for being courageous enough to pick this book up, read it and in the process discover what has been holding back your happiness. I have come to realize every time God brings more freedom and healing into my life, I have to share it. It is a part of my purpose. I am telling what I have come to understand is my business and God's business.

We sometimes want to protect those who have hurt us, and in the process of doing that, we become victims over and over again. Being free is personal and others may not understand or agree just how we become free. This is perfectly fine. Healing is personal. Finding our happiness is personal. We must give ourselves permission to dig deep within, dust off the cobwebs of our heart and find the person hidden under the pain. We deserve it.

All your tears, God has heard. Yes our tears have a sound. The have a sound of pain, frustration, betrayal, unworthiness and much more. God cares about each one of your tears because to Him it means we are in need of Him. He has the healing balm in His love to take all the pain away. He has not forgotten you.

All the betrayal, God has seen. He is not blind to those who have betrayed you. As you go through your journey to face the betrayal, the biggest step you will take is to Own Your Truth in the relationships. Own your truth that you drew a certain caliber of person to you because you were broken and needed to be loved. Yes, it is a hard pill to swallow but a necessary one in order to step out of the victim coat and onto a victor stage.

What others have done is what they have done, but what were we needing them to do for us because we are wounded and they could not fulfill? Those questions must be answered by us and for us before we can ever take the chains of the past off our lives.

Breathe, Baby girl!

You are braver than you ever believed. Do you know how strong you have had to be in order to live through everything that life has thrown at you? Yes, you lived through it. Now it is time for you to THRIVE! Yes, sister THRIVE. You were never meant to settle in life. You can lift your head up above the water that is your life. You can see that although you may feel you are sinking, there is land for you to rest your feet on. Swim Baby Girl, swim for your life and stand on the ground of support, love and strength that has always been available to you.

My story may not be your story or it may just be a reflection of it. My prayer is that you are empowered by what you are able to see God doing in my life and see a morsel of what is available to you. You are to do even greater in your walk with God.

I can see you now. You are smiling from the heart that once only knew pain because you have allowed God entry into your broken chambers. You are finding your voice in the midst of the broken pieces that is your heart. You are breathing a sigh of relief. You are giving yourself permission to face the very wounds that you ran from all your life. I Am so proud of you sis. I am giving you a standing ovation for being brave and courageous in your own story

Breathe Baby Girl!

This is not the end of your story, in fact, it is just the beginning. Others are waiting for you to step into who God called you to be. They need you to find your voice. In doing so they can receive from you what only you can speak into their lives because of your story. You are stepping onto your own stage and declaring freedom.

As your wounds are opened it will be tempting to shut down again and close the door. I remember that pain. Believe me God will be with you. You will look back and ask yourself, "When did I get brave enough not to run?" I asked myself the same question just in another way. Make a decision to stand through the struggles and emotions that opening the door of your heart to God will require. You call on God for the strength to stand and not run. I believe you can do this.

So as we end our journey together for right now, I would love to hear from you. If you enjoyed reading my story, that is fine. However, my greatest prayer will be to hear from you sharing how this book changed your life. I want to hear how you gave yourself permission to uncover your happiness. I want to hear from you because your story is touching mine. You matter to me, and I want to know walking in vulnerability and obedience to God has helped another sister to Find Her Voice and Stand in Her Power.

God bless, sissy. You are my sister from another mother. God did not allow my parents to give me a birth sister, but He has made sure that I am not without many sisters. You are One of them!

Love you much

You Sister Friend, xoxo

Lynette M. Bradshaw

Reflection:

I AM Declarations

I AM BRAVER THAN I HAVE BELIEVED

I AM SMART

I AM NOT ALONE

I AM LOVED

I AM COURAGEOUS

I AM NOT A VICTIM

I AM GIVING MYSELF PERMISSION TO THRIVE

I AM FREE

I AM HEALED

I AM WHOLE

I AM MORE THAN ENOUGH

I AM FINDING MY VOICE

I AM STRONG

I AM A GOOD PERSON

I AM CONFIDENT

I AM OWNING MY TRUTH

Other Work by This Author

Available at www.Amazon.com for Paperback and Kindle and www.RestoreHerWorth.com for Signed Copies (paperback only)

About the Author

Lynette Bradshaw (Pen name: Lynette M. Bradshaw) was born and raised in Natchez, Mississippi. She is the daughter of Ms. Josie Owens and the late Mr. Charles Owens. She is the oldest of three children. She moved to Dallas, Texas a few years after graduating high school.

She is the mother of Jarrius, Derrick, Adriel, Charity and her late son, Aarron. She was married for 20 years and is now divorced. She is an artist, author, speaker, the self-worth ignitor and a coach. She has been a professional photographer for 12 years (at the time of this writing). She works in the medical field currently. Her passions are singing and empowering other woman.

In 2013, she stepped into her purpose and began Restore Her Worth. Restore Her Worth empowers woman and girls to know their worth. Under the umbrella of Restore Her Worth, she leads seminars to assist women in finding their voice.

In July 2016, God gave her a vision to start the, "Who Am I, Really? Movement," to assist women and girls to dig deeper within themselves so they may know who they *Really* are underneath the pain, shame and silence.

In 2016, she decided to become a coach. As a result of working with Lynette, women uncover who they really are underneath their pain, shame and silence... They discover their Worth, Value and Voice as they find the courage in owning their truths...Breaking the cycle of toxic relationships as they face their "Why' and step into their POWER...

Download your complimentary EBook and Audio, "Who Am I, Really and join me in my Private Facebook Group http://bit.ly/1U8lLKW

Contact Info:

Lynette M. Bradshaw

P O BOX 381322

Duncanville, Texas 75138-1322

Office: 469-454-0556

www.RestoreHerWorth.com

Email: Lynette@RestoreHerWorth.com

 @ RestoreHerWorth

 @ RestoreHerWorth

 @ RestoreHerWorth

 @ RestoreHerWorth

www.ingramcontent.com/pod-product-compliance
Lightning Source LLC
Chambersburg PA
CBHW051425090426
42737CB00014B/2835